To Persia, With Love

By Kenneth S. Oster, D. Min.
with
Dorothy Minchin-Comm, Ph.D.

Pacific Press Publishing Association
Mountain View, California
Omaha, Nebraska
Oshawa, Ontario

Dedicated

to all beginners—especially those bold, bright spirits who in pioneer times planted God's truth in faraway places.

Copyright 1980 by
Pacific Press Publishing Association
Litho in United States of America
All Rights Reserved
Library of Congress Catalog Card No. 79-90022
ISBN 0-8163-0368-1
Cover illustration by Tim Mitoma

Preface

Throughout the thirty-five years of their foreign mission service Frank and Florence Oster were urged many times to write an account of their pioneer work in Persia and Turkey. With this purpose in mind, they kept faithful diaries. Upon returning to Persia after their first furlough in 1922, they were imprisoned in Russia and the police confiscated their entire ten-year collection of day-by-day accounts of their experiences. Unwilling to rely upon fallible human memory, they concluded that the story could never be written and gave up the idea.

Another hitherto unthought-of source of documentation, however, remained. In 1963 when Florence's sister, Mrs. Vandella Woodruff, died in Ventura Estates, California, it became Florence's lot to care for her sister's property. While looking through an old steamer trunk one afternoon, she discovered a large bundle of personal letters. To her amazement she recognized her own handwriting on them. Vandella had saved every letter she had ever received from Florence, beginning with the day of the Oster's wedding in London in 1913! Thus all of those first-hand experiences, hot from the front line of mission action, had been preserved for half a century.

As soon as I heard of this discovery, I sent Mother a tape recorder with instructions to read all of the letters aloud and record on tape the experiences of the early days which the letters recalled to her memory. Many more stories never before written down were thus added to the collection. So from those letters and tape transcriptions we have been able to reconstruct those early days of mission work in Queen Esther's land—days which are a mosaic of sorrow and joy, hardship and victory.

And now, almost a life-span later, the work in that ancient land remains unfinished, and the challenge is even greater than before. The Lord should have come long before this, and it is in the interest of bringing that day yet closer that we recount this story.

Long-forgotten Persia has today become modern, politically explosive Iran. The world oil shortage, the deposition of a king who traced his throne back to that of Cyrus the Great, and the burning issues of liberty under a religious government—all of these crises have caused the name of Iran, through the news media, to sweep through the world. The prospects for reaching this vital part of the Moslem world for Christ are just opening up. Frank, Florence, and others of that pioneer missionary generation have laid down their burdens in this ancient land. How God's work shall be finished in Iran remains in the hands of the new pioneers, working under the blessing of divine Providence.

Kenneth S. Oster
Shiraz, Iran
March 1979.

Some Historical Background

Ever since the caravans began to follow the famous silk route between China and Europe, Persia has been a place where East met West. The long camel trains passed under the shadow of the Bisitun rock, on which are inscribed the exploits of Darius the Great; and then they came into Persia's covered bazaars, where shrewd merchants bartered the sophisticated merchandise of Europe for the exotic silks, spices, precious metals, and gems of the East.

But more important than the trafficking of goods was the exchange of ideas. One Persian scientist created the sundial, and another built one of the first observatories—all in the tradition of the Magi who centuries earlier had studied the heavens, followed the Star, and found the Christ. The physician Avicenna used breadmold organisms to treat difficult wounds. Sir Alexander Fleming about 1000 years later restudied the antibiotic properties of this same organism, Penicillium, and brought life and healing to millions. Persian scholars have adventured down many obscure, intellectual paths far in advance of their European contemporaries.

The name *Iran* (land of the Aryans) is derived from the successive waves of Aryans who moved into the Persian plateau about 1500 B.C. The newcomers split into two main groups, the Medes and Persians, both conspicuously mentioned in the Bible.

The more advanced Medes settled principally in the northwest. They achieved a high civilization with their vast wealth in horses, cattle, sheep, goats, and watchdogs, along with wheeled wagons and military chariots. Moreover, they also knew how to write. By the seventh century B.C. they had established an empire which included the Persians, who had settled farther south in the province of *Fars* (or *Pars*). From their splendid capital at Ecbatana (modern Hamadan) they threatened—with some assistance from the Babylonians—even the Assyrians of Nineveh.

Meanwhile the Persian branch of the Aryans in the east began to gain supremacy over their northern overlords. The Neo-Babylon of Nebuchadnezzar's and Belshazzar's time had a dominant role in world politics, and Daniel describes the power play which brought these great kingdoms into collison (Daniel 2-5). A Persian chief, Cyrus, established the Achaemenid (*Hakhamanish*) Dynasty, naming it after his own family clan. Later his grandson, Cyrus the Great, reigned first in Persia for twenty years and then went on to destroy Babylon (539 B.C.) and become one of the most dynamic men in history. One of God's prophets hailed his advent on the world stage in some of the most lofty utterances to be found in the Bible (Isaiah 44:28-45:4).

Through a series of providential circumstances, Cyrus came to the throne, captured the Median capital, overthrew their empire, and then united all of modern Iran under his single rule. He established one of the world's first multi-nation states, one in which the rights of the diverse groups remained inviolate and their laws and customs respected.

His successor Cambyses held the great world empire together for a few years. Tradition states he was killed in an accident but his successor, Darius, states that he took his own life. Darius I (522-486 B.C.) issued the second decree for the return of the Jews to Jerusalem (Ezra 6) and saw to the completion of the building of the temple by Ezra (515 B.C.). Next came Xerxes (486-465 B.C.), the Ahasuerus of the Bible, who took the Jewess Esther as his queen in 478 B.C. Artaxerxes (464-423 B.C.) issued the third and last decree to reestablish the Jewish state—an act which marked the starting point of Daniel's 2300-year prophecy (Daniel 8:14).

At the height of its prosperity the Persian Empire covered most of the modern Middle East, with the exception of the Arabian Peninsula. It extended from the Indus River well up into southern Russia, and included part of Greece, Turkey, Cyprus, modern Egypt, and present-day Libya. The empire collapsed in 331 B.C. before the advancing armies of Alexander the Great. What the prophet Daniel does not explain, however, is that while the Greeks occupied Persian lands they were themselves, in fact, conquered. During the Seleucid Period, Persian culture and custom overcame the Hellenistic victors, and through the Greeks Persian civilization spread into the West and Europe. The military takeover proved to be but one portion of the two-way conquest.

The Parthians were a relatively less-civilized Aryan tribe of what is now northeast Iran. In 250 B.C. they ousted the successors of the Greek Seleucus who had ruled Iran for more than four centuries. Again the dominant Persian culture inexorably transformed the invaders. In the third century of the Christian era Ardashir, a local leader, overthrew his Parthian overlord, Artabanus (A.D. 224), and established the Sāssānian Empire, which survived until the Moslem invasion of A.D. 641.

Like their predecessors, the Arab Moslems conquered Persia. But the Islamization of Iran became, in effect, an Iranization of Islam—a phenomenon to which even Arab scholars admit. (See the writings of al-Masudi and Ibn-Khaldun.) The mainstream of Islamic orthodoxy (*Sunni*) metamorphosed into *Shi'ism*, a distinctively Iranian brand of belief. Politically Persia rendered lip service to the reigning caliphs of Damascus and Baghdad, but the country soon became restive. A number of small native dynasties appeared in various parts of Persia, some enjoying considerable power and prestige.

Then came the greatest calamity ever to hit the Middle East, the Mongol invasions (A.D. 1218-1224). Genghis Khan, followed later by *Timūr* (Tamerlane) ravaged Persia's rich cities and almost obliterated her arts and sciences. Somehow Persian culture weathered this barbarous invasion and lived on to shine again with new luster. Shah Abbas the Great (1587-1629) of the Safavi Dynasty restored his land to a prosperity it had not known for centuries. His splendid capital of Sultanabad (now Arāk) still inspires today's tourist with awe and admiration. Under his patronage the famous carpet-making industry expanded into a world-renowned art. Silks, velvets, and brocades filled the bazaars and testified to luxurious tastes. And fine architectural designs with delicate metalwork, ceramics, and tiles displayed a high-water mark in Persian art.

Nadir Shah, the "Napoleon of Persia," ruled for sixty tumultuous years and then gave way to the peaceful Zand Dynasty. Meanwhile, Europe had emerged from her Dark Ages and swept into a renaissance of learning and exploration. Humanism made Europeans acutely aware of nations and people in faraway places. This fascination, of course, grew into political rivalry as the competition for colonies and trade escalated. Spheres of influence evolved, and sanctions and concessions were imposed upon decadent and/or dormant countries. Unmerciful exploitation abounded.

In Iran the Qājārs became the first to bear the brunt of Russian and British imperialism. The hand of colonialism lay heavy until 1925, when Reza Shah, founder of the Pahlavi Dynasty, took vigorous measures to launch Iran on the road to prosperity and into a respectable place in the family of modern nations.

Many of the life experiences of Frank and Florence depicted in this account have portrayed privations and difficulties of pioneer days. To leave the reader with only this viewpoint on Persia would be to totally distort the picture of conditions in modern Iran. Now many of these obstacles have entirely disappeared. The new mission recruit, for instance, no longer enters the country through a series of caravansary stops. He flies into Tehran's beautiful Mehrabad (Loveland) Airport aboard a Boeing 747 on any of the great world airlines. If he chooses, he can be whisked off in a limousine to spend his first night in the Royal Tehran Hilton. Perhaps he wants something less extravagant—the choice is wide open in that great city of four million people.

In any case, wherever he is, if he's very lucky he *might* hear the before-dawn, rhythmic tinkle of camel bells coming from some far-off desert place, as a caravan moves into a marketplace. The modernization program has still retained a few colorful, ethnic trappings. By and large, however, produce reaches Tehran in air-conditioned trucks, which roll along over a 40,000-kilometer system of roads, a quarter of which are first-class asphalt pavement. This boon, along with the air and rail connections, gives Iran a communication and transport network unequaled anywhere in Asia. The visitor, therefore, finds the department stores and supermarkets stocked with imported goods. Less expensive local merchandise is, however, more than adequate. Staple grains and a complete range of garden vegetables and fruit are grown in abundance. The quality of a succulent Persian cucumber or a delectable 100-pound melon is hard to match anywhere. Such variety is gleaned from mountains, desert, and sea. There are peaches and pears from the Zagros Mountains and dates from the desert. And in every hamlet one can find nuts—almonds to pistachios (the *pistah* of Persian origin)—to say nothing of all the other savory tidbits peculiar to the land of the Aryans. In the fields of aesthetics, the Iranian gardens have made their contributions as well. The rose, narcissus, and jasmine still carry the names which reveal their Persian origins.

The country's rich mineral resources, of course, have bedazzled the world far more than any other natural feature. They have long fed the exploitative needs and interests of the rest of the world. The Persian oil story goes back to 1901, when the Qājār rulers gave the British a sixty-year monopoly on Iranian oil. The five northern provinces came under Russian influence. The Anglo-Persian Oil Company formed in 1908 became Anglo-Iranian Oil in deference to the name-change of the country in 1935, and finally British Petroleum. After long disputes the oil industry was nationalized in 1951 and came under an international amalgam of interests. In becoming the world's fourth largest oil producer, Iran has gained wealth, status—and problems—which no other attainment could possibly have brought her so rapidly.

After long centuries of intellectual starvation, the Iranians now surpass most nations in the world in their passion for education. Thousands of primary and secondary schools are augmented by vocational schools; teacher-training colleges; and eight well-equipped, expertly staffed universities. The army's "Literacy Corps" sends young men to teach in rural areas as an option to regular military service. Within twenty-five years Iran has moved from a medieval kind of decadence into the twentieth century, thereby inheriting both its marvelous advantages and massive problems.

The record of Christian missions in Persia is quite another story. Islam, vigorously alive and militant, has from its beginnings elicited a level of fervor and loyalty among its people that has been seen only occasionally in other religions. Here the missionary task has proved to be perhaps the most difficult in the whole world.

For the first fifty years of Seventh-day Adventist work in Persia (beginning in 1911) there were a total of twenty-nine missionaries (twelve European, seventeen Americans in the country). Frank and Florence Oster worked there alone for eleven years (1914-1925). Obviously the scourge of World War I had much to do with that situation. By the summer of 1933, however, ten missionaries were serving the field at the same time, the great depression notwithstanding. The war years of 1941-1945 brought another low, with only three missionaries in Iran, but immediately after the end of World War II eleven families returned to Persia. Since then the numbers have fluctuated, depending on the temperature of the continuing "Middle East Problem" and its reflections in Iran.

Just how the gospel is to reach the Moslem millions still remains a daily challenge. Kenneth Oster is his father's evangelistic successor in Iran, but he has transferred the emphasis from Armenian Christian work to witnessing to the Moslem population. His method has been based on two premises. The first is that "it is *impossible,*" as Ellen White says, "for men and women, while under the power of sinful, health-destroying, brain-enervating habits, to appreciate sacred truth."—*Counsels on Health,* p. 21. Consequently he has used health lectures, nutrition education, and the world-famous Five-Day Plan to Stop Smoking to useful ends.

Second, instead of accentuating the differences between Islam and Christianity (which undeniably are many), Dr. Oster has emphasized the very striking similarities, in an appeal to the intellectuals. Correlations between the Old Testament and the Koran are much more than just accidental. In his recent book written in the Farsi language, *Cosmic Perspective of God and Man,* (Beirut, Lebanon: Middle East Press, June, 1978), Dr. Oster has defined these issues in what, after sixty-seven years of missionary endeavor in Persia, is actually the first direct address to Moslems.

Contents

An International Wedding 13
Honeymoon in Transit 21
Maragha Housekeeping 32
One Woman's World 39
Living With Terror 47
The Lord Gives, and— 56
Trials and Triumphs 64
The End of an Era 74
First Furlough 82
Shadows of the Russian Revolution 94
Barrier Breakthrough 104
A Turn of the Tide 115
Celebrations of the New Look 128
A Swiss Detour 140
Tests—the Small and the Great 149
Call to Turkey 159
Into the Storm 170
A Destiny Fulfilled 183
Epilogue 189

Frank and Florence Oster, taken on their wedding day in London, England, September 1, 1913. Their honeymoon trip—off to Persia!

An International Wedding

Closing the door of her third-floor classroom, Florence White started down the steep wooden stairs on the west side of the administration building. Automatically she chose the "girls' side", for, although she had become a faculty member now, old habits learned in her own student days died hard. And the regulations here at South Lancaster Academy were just as conservative as those back at Walla Walla College where she had graduated just about this time three years ago. This administration building had two stairways to segregate student traffic, one for the boys and one for the girls. That way no one had to worry about stragglers lingering on the landings or dallying in the dark, narrow angles of the stairwells.

But Florence wasn't thinking about discipline problems today. She wasn't even thinking about her pupils. Some days, under the heavy pressures of the school program, she wondered what really was "normal" about her job—but then the training of elementary school teachers had for some reason always been known as the "normal course," as far back as anyone could remember. No, this afternoon as she stood on the porch of the classroom building, she could look past the dormitory and past Elder Haskell's big boxy house all the way to the church.

Ah, yes, the church! She walked down the broad flight of porch steps, heading in that direction. The fragrance of lilacs and hyacinths drifted across her path. The miracle of early summer had happened again in Massachusetts, and it was enough to set any girl to dreaming.

At Prescott Street she stopped and looked up at the windows of the union conference office building. Father would probably be late coming home again tonight. His duties as union conference president often kept his office lights burning at night long after almost all of the bedroom windows along the street were dark.

But the church! She looked at it again. Trim and white, it stood among the new spring-green trees. The clear-paned windows and slender spire fitted into the best traditions of the Puritan forefathers of New England. Florence smiled to herself with satisfaction—this was going to be a very lovely place to have the wedding. By the end of this summer of 1913 she would be Mrs. Frank Oster. Mrs. Florence Oster—the words sounded very pleasant together.

And perhaps a letter from Frank waited for her. She hurried across the street to where one little store with a post office made up the entire "commercial center" of the town of South Lancaster. She sifted through her letters quickly, looking for that dear familiar handwriting and the foreign stamps. None from him! But, of course, Persia *was* a very long way off, and communications could be slow and irregular.

Florence sauntered on down the tree-shaded street toward home. As she opened the front door, she could smell the come-hither aroma of a batch of mother's bread.

"That you, Florence?" Mother's voice came, not unexpectedly, from the back of the house.

"Yes, Mother." Florence detoured through the living room and into the kitchen. She perched on a stool and waited to see what was behind that extra gleam she saw in her mother's eye. And didn't she catch a note of excitement in her voice too? "What is it? Come—you've got news."

Mrs. White dried her hands on her apron and sat down at the kitchen table. "Yes, news indeed." Drawing a deep breath, she launched directly into her story. "Father had a letter from the General Conference this morning. They are asking him to go to South Africa—to establish a new union there."

"South Africa! When?" Florence's mind raced off in a hundred directions at once.

"This summer—just as soon as we can get ready." Her mother barely paused for a breath. "And there's more."

"More?" Florence's mind reeled.

"Yes, Lulu and Omer are being called to go to South Africa too."

Florence tried to take it all in. Africa would be a big change for her sister and brother-in-law, from their pastorate in Montreal, Quebec—but what an adventure for their children. "Why, mother, we'll all be going off here and there, scattered all over the world." Florence's voice trembled.

"It will be a big change, dear," Mrs. White stood up and bent to kiss her daughter before she turned the bread out of the pans and oiled the golden crusts. "But don't worry, the wedding can still be arranged. You'll see."

The W. B. Whites had held a number of positions of responsibility in the Seventh-day Adventist Church, so moves here or there had become rather a family "way of life."

Still, the timing of this one was unusual, at least as far as Florence was concerned. Ever since she had promised to marry Frank Oster, she had known that she was going to be a missionary in Persia. *Inshallah* (if God wills it)—that was an Arabic phrase Frank had already introduced her to. They would be the pioneer missionaries in Persia. But now the whole family was being scattered to the ends of the earth. Well, older sister Vandella would still be at home, on the west coast—kind of an anchor point while the rest wandered.

When Father White came home that night, the family settled on a very practical suggestion. Why not ask Frank to meet them in England and have the wedding there instead of having him come all the way back to the United States only to return to Persia? And, of course, Father could still perform the wedding ceremony just as planned. And several members of the family would be present as well.

Late that evening Florence climbed the stairs and hurried to her room. Then she flung herself down into the old overstuffed mohair chair to collect her thoughts. The pretty image of the little white South Lancaster church began to blur into a rapid procession of exotic scenes—castles, misty English meadows, and an English garden. She got up and took a large white box off the top of a wardrobe shelf. Lifting off the lid and opening the layers of tissue paper, she fingered the silky, pale-blue folds of her wedding dress. She patted down the high collar and deep lace yoke. So, she thought, she would be wearing this somewhere in England and not in the little church up the street! The details to be attended to in the remaining weeks suddenly multiplied into thousands, it seemed, compounded now by this abrupt change of plans.

"As God directs and wills it" she mused, with a very tangible impression that this prayer, this attitude would mold her destiny and shape all the years of her life to come. Standing at the window and looking down on the lights and shadows of Prescott Street under the full spring moon, she said her first farewell to this lovely spot that had been her home for the past two years. Then she thought of Frank, a bachelor missionary now for nearly four years. She would marry this man she hadn't seen in all of that time!

Their friendship back at Walla Walla College had been casual, and, because of prevailing regulations, it had really had only a public side to it. After Frank and his friend Henry Dirksen had left for Persia in 1909, however, the steady letter-writing had begun. So now, courtesy of the International Post Office, Frank and Florence had come to know each other as two individual persons—two people who had decided they wanted to marry each other.

She had first met Frank at the Foreign Mission Band which Professor Harry Washburn had organized. She remembered that night when she and Frank sat side by side and signed the pledge cards which read: "If God permits, it is my desire to become a foreign missionary."

Well, God had not only permitted, He seemed to have been quite definite about the matter. Frank and Henry already had gone to Persia. Other friends had also departed for mission service—Harold Oberg to Korea, and Allen Ham to China. With the new vision of foreign missions that had come after the General Conference session of 1901, a number of young men had been chosen for overseas service. The brethren certainly must have had access to all those pledge cards which had been signed in the colleges, Florence thought. And now it would be her turn to go. There had been no clear arrangement about the length of the term of service in the mission field, but everyone seemed to have gone out with the understanding that it was a lifetime commitment.

Florence opened the bottom bureau drawer and pulled out a box of letters from Frank. She took out the last letter she'd had from him and re-read it. He had been alone in Persia for over a year, and though he didn't speak of it directly, Florence knew that he had times of great loneliness. Yes, he needed her. Henry Dirksen had stayed only a year. He had found language study a real strain, and the results of all their labors had been so small that he had ultimately capitulated to discouragement.

The night hours wore on, but now time meant nothing to Florence. She looked at the bundle of letters for 1909. That was the year Frank and Henry had left home for Europe. They had stopped in Washington, D.C., to attend the General Conference session. Ellen G. White had preached, and Frank had counted it a special privilege to have been there, for, considering Mrs. White's advanced age, it might well be her last message to such a group.

There had been a surprise that year when Frank applied for his U.S. passport. For the first time he discovered that he wasn't a citizen of the United States. When his family had emigrated from Switzerland to America, he had been only three years old. Somehow in the documentation and processing of the family's citizenship papers, his name had been omitted, so he remained a Swiss citizen.

"It's no doubt possible for you to get a U.S. passport," Elder Spicer, the secretary of the General Conference, had advised, "but since you're going to work in the European Division, why don't you just retain your Swiss citizenship?"

Swiss or otherwise, it didn't help much. Persia smoldered with unrest which bordered on civil war, and was granting visas to no one. For several months Frank and Henry had stayed at the Friedensau Industrial School, as it was then called, in Germany. They learned physical therapy and other practical studies. Impatient as they were to get on to their appointment in the East, the processes of bureaucracy could not be hastened. They even had time to conduct a few tent efforts in Germany before they finally went to the language study center in Russia. Since Russia had retained control of Persia's northwestern province of Azerbaijan, this seemed the most likely way to get in.

Then came 1910. Frank had spent that whole year in Baku, Russia, with a contingent of pioneer missionaries preparing for active, frontline service. Just across the Caspian Sea lay Persia. Frank settled down with a Persian teacher to begin mastering the speech and script of the ancient Aryan race. He had made some good friends there too—especially his roommates, Jacques and

Osol. These two men were both sent into exile as a result of mass arrests of Protestants. Frank was present at a secret mountain baptism conducted by Brother Osol, who was arrested for doing what he believed was right. At that time he was working as a district leader in Tiflis. The courageous, fur-hatted, bear-cloaked Seventh-day Adventist evangelist lived only a few weeks after reaching Siberia. Jacques, who later escaped, authored the book *Escape From Siberian Exile.*

The most thrilling and historic year had been 1911. Florence had memorized the date as well as Frank himself had—May 11. On that day Frank and Henry entered Persia, the very first resident Seventh-day Adventists to go into the ancient land of Queen Esther. They established themselves among the Armenians in the city of Urmia. Relative peace and order prevailed under Russian supervision, and the men devoted themselves to further language study. Attempts at opening Bible studies were generally disappointing—except for the case of Captain Sperling, a Russian army officer. He came to the studies with a keen interest and a colorful band of Russian Cossacks who always attended him as bodyguards. The baptism of Captain Sperling and his wife Erica made them the firstfruits of Adventism in Persia. Of course they weren't Persians, but Frank rejoiced in this first victory for the gospel nonetheless.

Florence had lived through all of these adventures with Frank by letter; now she was on the point of becoming part of them—and they of her. Closing her box of letters, she finally went to bed a little before dawn.

From then on the weeks disappeared at an alarming rate, filled with shopping, packing, and sewing. Two families going to Africa, and a bride to Persia! Her sister, Vandella, gave her a sewing machine for a wedding gift. Probably nothing else could have been a more practical and sensible piece of luggage to carry into Persia.

At last travel arrangements had been finalized. A cable went off to Frank telling him to meet their ship in Liverpool on August 15!

The Atlantic crossing gave the families a chance to relax and get ready for the explosion of responsibility about to overtake them all. Florence enjoyed the sunny hours on deck—precious times with her parents and other members of the family. A long separation was about to begin—just how long no one could venture to guess.

Standing at the rail with the breeze whipping through her hair, she watched the steamer breaking waves in the deep, indigo-blue water and making swirling patterns of snowy foam streak through the smooth, dark eddies. The sight thrilled her—giving birth to high thoughts and deep feelings.

There were many other things to wonder about too. In four years had Frank changed? Had she? What would it be like to be together all the time? She knew that she wanted to marry him. They both felt assured that this was God's will for them. But still, a "paper romance" can have a few drawbacks. Things now were certainly going to be, well—different!

Then, that Friday morning of August 15 came. The ship steamed northeast, in toward the gray coast of England, and then the harbor materialized against the city background of Liverpool. Florence had no plans to miss a thing. As the warehouses and docks seemed to move closer, she strained her eyes to see the crowds on the wharf. The ship edged up to the pier, and then she saw *him!* The engines churned in reverse and then stopped, as the great hull slipped smoothly into her moorings.

He stood right below her looking unspeakably handsome, Florence thought. And so dignified in his smart new hat and tweedy English suit. His fine-featured face could scarcely hold his smile, it spread so wide. In his hands he carried a big bouquet of pink carnations and lily-of-the-valley. For her! So, he would begin by "saying it with flowers."

What happened between that first magic instant and the moment when they were at last together was of no consequence, and Florence scarcely remembered how they all got off the ship. It was enough that Frank took her hands in his, and she read the deep affection in his eyes when he said, "Floss! You've come!" Never a man of flowery speech, in those words Frank had said it all.

Two weeks remained before the wedding—two weeks filled with activity. Some of the time they spent in sightseeing. Kind friends offered their home as wedding headquarters for Florence's family. When Florence opened her box and shook out the soft folds of her wedding dress, somehow South Lancaster already seemed a thousand years behind her. New things were happening so fast that she could scarcely keep up with them.

But then—and it seemed so sudden—she and Frank stood together in front of a bay window overlooking an English garden in London. "And now, solemnly promising before God and in the presence of these witnesses, wilt thou, Frank Frederick Oster, have this woman, Florence Genevieve White, to be thy lawfully wedded wife—?" Elder White looked tenderly upon his two children as he pronounced the quaint, sweet words of the vows over them. And so they married on that September day in 1913.

Reception, last-minute messages, admonitions, tears, and laughter—and then they were off to Waterloo Station. As they hurried through the huge concourse, Florence wondered if they looked as newly married as they actually were. Family and friends helped them aboard the train to Southhampton, which would make connections with the boat to cross the English Channel. Then, with the very last farewells, they were away.

Frank and Florence sat down at the window and watched the station platform slip away beside them; then the railway yards loomed into view. The train worked up to a fast, clackety-clack rhythm, punctuated by the switches on the tracks. Soon sooty old London gave way to the cool greens of the southern countryside.

The couple looked at one another and smiled—deep smiles. "Mr. and Mrs. Frank Oster," Florence thought to herself. It had happened! The beginning of their honeymoon, and they were off to Persia.

Honeymoon in Transit

On the first morning of their stay in Hamburg, headquarters of the European Division, Frank awoke with a great conviction. "Floss, we'll go and see Elder Conradi first thing when he comes to his office today. I have something to ask him." He sat up in bed.

"What's that?" Florence felt sure that whatever it was, she wouldn't be able to change his mind about it.

"I'm a married man now." Frank grinned and squared his shoulders. "I think I should have a raise in salary."

Florence gasped. "You mean you'll go and ask him for it, just like that?"

"Just like that, my dear. Just like that." Frank smiled down at her.

"But he's the division superintendent. I mean, maybe you'll get it automatically and won't have to ask for it," Florence cast about for some more graceful way to take up the matter.

"Well, I just want to be sure," Frank said. "Getting nine dollars a week is hardly a lavish income."

"And, of course, two really don't live as cheaply as one, in spite of what the old proverb says," Florence replied. She had been earning twenty-one dollars a week in South Lancaster, so Frank's desire for a raise certainly didn't seem unduly extravagant.

Later that morning, as the newlyweds approached the office building, their pace slackened a little. "Well, it's good that you're with me," Frank mused. "It should help me make my point."

Florence felt even more hesitant now than she had at the start. But when Elder Conradi opened his door and invited them in, she took heart. He seemed very gracious and cordial, every inch a gentleman. She relaxed a bit as she sat down.

When the social preliminaries had concluded, Frank began. "Ah, Elder Conradi, we were—uh—we were wondering . . ."

"Yes, young man? What is it that you have on your mind?" the division superintendent asked.

"Well—er," Frank seemed to have lost some of the confidence he'd had back in their room an hour or so ago. "You see, now that I have a wife, do you suppose that I—I mean, we—we could have an increase in salary?"

There! It was out. Florence felt the blood rush to her face, and she looked at her shoes.

"Well, now. Let me see." Elder Conradi reached for the ledger and slowly and very deliberately examined the accounts. Frank and Florence glanced uneasily at each other. After several minutes, the older man looked up, and his eyes steadily met those of the waiting couple. He leaned back in his chair with an air of expansive generosity. "Yes, your request does seem quite reasonable. From now on your salary will be nine dollars fifty cents per week."

A heavy silence hung in the room and threatened to lengthen itself to the point of embarrassment. Finally Frank collected himself sufficiently enough to say, "Well, thank you, Elder Conradi." They stood up and shook hands with Elder Conradi and turned toward the door. "We appreciate your help," Frank added.

Once outside, Frank spoke first. "Hah!" He shook his head as if someone had hit it with a bat. "I see my bride is worth 50 cents!" He stared at Florence in disbelief.

She choked down her suprise and patted him on the arm. "It's all right, Frank. Just so long as *you* think I'm worth more than that to you. We'll manage."

And manage they would. High hopes, strong courage, excellent health—they had all this going for them. What was more, they had unreservedly dedicated themselves to a lifetime of service in Persia.

At no time had Florence considered that money would be a big issue in their minds. Of course, they would need some, but she hadn't supposed that they would start out with it playing quite this minor a role in their lives. Still, she could think of many things of greater consequence than the amount of their income.

As they traveled steadily east, and as she had said all her

good-byes to her family in England, she thought more than ever about the family reunion in heaven. She felt a new urgency to be there. She seemed so far from perfection. So she and Frank now prayed together often—for each other, for the family at home and elsewhere, and for their work in Persia.

Upon arriving in Warsaw, Poland, the couple experienced the first of many delays. From Warsaw to Persia they anticipated a trip of not more than three weeks. They were eager to be on their way. But Frank spent days trudging from this office to that securing the necessary permits and travel papers.

Sundown came on what Florence hoped would be the last day. She had been peering out of the window of their hotel room for a long time. Frank was unusually late—and then she saw him coming. Would he have good news this time? Too impatient to wait, she ran out into the hall to meet him. "Did you get the visas?"

"Well, yes and no." Frank opened the door and ushered her into their room. "I've been issued the visa for Russia, but the Persian consul told me to come back tomorrow."

"Tomorrow? But what about our train reservations for tomorrow morning?" Florence felt a wave of disappointment sweep over her. Delays seemed interminable.

"I shall have to cancel them," Frank said. "But don't worry, Floss. He put his arm around her as they watched the setting sun silhouette the Warsaw skyline in an amber glow. "I'll make reservations for the afternoon train instead. God knows what we're supposed to do. We can't get too anxious and run ahead of Him, you know."

And, true enough, the next afternoon they were on the train—visas in hand—speeding toward the Russian border. The Polish countryside streaked past their window until darkness blotted it all out. Frank pulled out his watch. "We'll have to be at the border before midnight in order to get the train into the Russian interior."

The hours passed. The rails kept humming away under them, but still they hadn't arrived at any known place. Florence yawned, and Frank pulled out his watch again. Sure enough, they weren't going to make it.

At last they arrived at the border—two hours late! When they had their luggage transferred, they walked over to the Russian side. Frank inquired about hotels. The stationmaster, sleepy and irritable, informed them that there were no hotels in town. He told them that he supposed they could sleep on the benches in the railroad station if they wanted to.

Thankful that it was autumn and not Russian mid-winter, they stretched out on the benches. When Frank couldn't sleep and decided to sit up, Florence pulled her coat around her, curled up, and used his lap for a pillow. She snatched just enough sleep to enable her to face the dawn with at least some degree of anticipation. Now another train would come. And no rushing to catch it either, for they were already there on the station platform when it steamed in!

It seemed that they were only well on their way when the train screeched to an abrupt stop. Frank leaned out of the window. "Something's going on up there," he said. "Let's go and see."

Something, indeed, was going on. "Oh," Florence cried. "See, it's a derailed train. O, Frank! How dreadful!" Splintered carriages lay about like matchwood. Men had been working for eight hours to clean up the carnage but were still far from finished. Forty-five people had been killed and 125 injured, they were told.

"Floss, this is the train that we were supposed to be on," Frank said quietly, "But—"

"But God detained us in Warsaw so we couldn't get on it," Florence finished for him. Suddenly she realized, almost as if for the first time, that God did have a time clock set for their lives. The management of it would have to be left to Him, always.

She felt faint at the sight of the wreckage. Some men were digging a long ditch, while others were piling up the dead like cordwood. Suddenly she realized the ditch would be the grave for all those who had been killed in the wreck. "Oh, Frank, can it be possible that all those bodies will be buried in a common grave? Don't they have any respect?"

"I'm afraid not, Floss," Frank's gentle voice calmed her. "And we could well have been among those going into that mass grave, had God not spared our lives."

"How terrible for all of those people." Florence's mind raced to the scores of homes which had been shattered all in an instant, when the train plunged off the rails. They were left with very sober thoughts.

There followed ten memorable days of travel in Russia, north of the Black Sea and down into the Caucasus Mountains. Carriages, street cars, and hotels were in short supply. Florence, along with Frank, who had already mastered the art, began to learn to sleep almost anywhere. One whole week passed when she did not even have a chance to take her clothes off. The days and the nights had to be spent *on* trains or waiting in stations *for* trains.

No sleepers (Pullmans) being available, the couple traveled second class, where they had the benefit of upholstered benches. Most of the passengers, of course, traveled third and fourth class. One look at fourth class was enough for Florence. Packed into the cars like cattle and with nothing to sit on, the people huddled together in groups on the floor, trying to keep warm.

Florence fervently thanked God for the comforts they had. She rejoiced too in the fact that despite all the irregularities in their lives, she felt well. She realized now that one of the best gifts she had to take with her was her good health.

Russia offered constant interest and surprises. To Florence it seemed that weapons abounded everywhere. People carried them as casually as umbrellas or walking sticks.

"Does *every* man in Russia carry a sword or a revolver?" she asked Frank one day.

"I don't know," Frank replied, "but I would guess that most of them do. If everyone else had one, I daresay you'd feel pretty insecure having nothing yourself—especially with self-protection left up to you. Did I ever tell you about the time I was arrested here?"

"Arrested? Whatever for?"

"Back in 1911 when Henry and I came through here on our first entry into Persia, I was just standing by the road near a riverbank. Someone told me the name of the river, and I was writing it down because I wanted to find it later on a map." Frank smiled at the recollection of his encounter with the law in Russia. "Two great fellows in leather boots collared me and wanted to take me to jail. They declared I was a spy!"

"Of course," Florence put in, "when they saw what you'd written on the paper, they could see that it was nothing."

"Well, not exactly. You see, neither of them could read English. It took some doing to talk myself out of that one. They were absolutely convinced that I was taking notes for their enemies." Frank chuckled.

Florence pondered on the amount of insecurity, suspicion, and anxiety that lay barely concealed beneath the surface of life here. "So I see it pays to walk circumspectly here at all times," she said.

"Always." Two years of living on the troubled crossroads to Asia had made Frank conscious of every move he made. "Someone's watching us all of the time—we may not know where, or who, but they are there."

When they reached Tiflis (now Tbilisi) both Frank and Florence felt that they had almost arrived. After all, there was Persia, just over on the other side of the mountains of Armenia. But something yet remained to try their patience to the limit—going through Russian customs! Familiar as he was with endless trips through consular offices, railway stations, and customhouses, Frank foresaw that this would be a prolonged episode.

"Relax, Floss. We're going to be here for a while, I'm afraid. Might as well look around and enjoy yourself," he told her.

So, early each morning Frank went off to the customhouse. The officers there were in no hurry at all, and they took great care to weigh and record every single item in the Osters' suitcases. They didn't miss a pencil, a handkerchief, or one pair of socks. The rest of the freight shipment proved to be equally fascinating to the customs officers—the cookstove and dishes Frank had bought for Florence in Germany; the little pump organ, that became a special novelty; and, of course, Florence's precious sewing machine.

The customs officers went through it all, methodically and deliberately, taking notes and apparently acquiring a whole liberal education from their investigation of the foreigners' goods. With so much at stake, Frank felt that he had to be present every hour that the doors of the customhouse stood open. Although he could do nothing to hurry up the dreary process, at least he could make sure that everything that came *out* of a trunk also went back *into* it when the examination and discussion of each item concluded.

Meanwhile, Florence tended to their little room in the hotel; wrote letters home, and strolled along the streets, taking in the many new sights and strange customs that engulfed her every waking hour. Sometimes it all left her nearly speechless.

The streets teemed with camels, oxcarts, and donkeys loaded with packs bigger than themselves. The camel drivers were a fierce-looking lot, wearing either turbans or tight-fitting skull caps. The long full-skirted coats covered their short trousers but not their great dirty old shoes. Long red sashes livened up the general drabness of the outfit and coordinated with the red henna with which they dyed their beards.

Florence learned to distinguish the women by their costumes. The modern ones chose Parisian styles and could not readily be differentiated from Americans. The Armenian women, however, were more distinctive with their long curled hair caught up by a flat little band on the top of the head. From this band a large white veil hung gracefully down the back. Over it all, they tied a black, three-cornered kerchief. The few Persian Moslem women walked with their faces completely veiled with a long black cloth that fell all the way to the floor, back and front. Florence studied those dark figures intently.

In the evenings Frank and Florence compared notes on the day's adventures. Frank's reports were quite materialistic. "I'm afraid we're going to have to pay a high duty on the sewing machine, and maybe the organ too," he remarked gloomily.

Florence, on the other hand, was always full of questions. "Why do the men all carry those strings of beads, fingering them all the time? I don't see the women with them. Are the men so much more pious, to be praying all the while?"

"Those aren't rosaries, Floss," Frank explained. "Those are their 'worry beads'!"

"Worry beads? What do you mean?"

"Oh, they fidget with them when they feel nervous, and it relieves their tension."

Florence laughed. "You mean a man's pacifier, then!"

"Yes, something like that." Frank stretched out his legs and yawned. "I'm *tired.*"

Florence knew how the hours—the days—wasted in the customhouse sorely vexed Frank's order-loving soul. He had a passion for precision and efficiency. Running her fingers through his hair, she bent to kiss him on the forehead. "Poor Frank!" she said. "If we can't go through customs soon, maybe I'll have to get you a string of worry beads!"

Frank pretended shock, reached up and pulled her down on his knee. "Not yet, Floss. Not yet. God knows all about our affairs. He won't lay on us more than we can bear."

Then at last, one cold November day, they got permission to leave Russia and go over into Persia. They had spent exactly one month in Tiflis getting through customs!

But now, with this task behind them, they boarded the train in high spirits, bound for the border town of Julfa (now Dzhulfa) on the northern bank of the Arāks River. Frank pointed out the peaks of Ararat, and they stopped briefly in Nakhichevan. "The Armenians have a tradition that says Noah founded this town," Frank said.

Florence looked at the sloping, pastured hillsides and tried to people them with Noah and his sons, planting their vineyard and tending their sheep. In any case, she got a sense of looking deep into the past, into scenes of unmeasured antiquity, into the beginnings of the world. She relished the new experience.

At Julfa they had to change trains. A newly constructed railroad bridge spanned the Arāks River here. Today it was alive on both ends with excitement. As the train edged onto the bridge, a forest of banners and flags moved ahead of it. "Whatever's going on here?" Florence looked out the window with astonishment.

A man across the aisle leaned over. "This is the ceremony for opening this new bridge," he explained.

Frank leaned out of the window and pulled Florence up beside him. Sure enough, the priests in their ceremonial robes picked their way gingerly across the ties as they walked ahead of the engine. Praying, chanting, and reciting, they dedicated the bridge and sought to turn aside the powers of misfortune. The celebration turned out to be a long one, but eventually the train did reach the other side. Frank and Florence had the distinction of being on the very first train ever to enter Persia.

At the station on the Persian side of the river, however, they had to get off. Here, for the present, the Persian railroad ended! But Florence didn't care. This was it! Persia at last! A wave of happy anticipation thrilled through her. Here they would set up their first home together and enter into their first work together. Their new life started right here and now in the station at the end, or was it the beginning of the Persian railway line.

From now on, they would travel by phaeton—a carriage drawn by horses, four abreast. The driver sat on a high seat in front with the passengers behind and below him.

There could be no possible way that Florence would ever forget her first night in Persia. At sundown they stopped at a caravansary, the "modern" equivalent of the desert caravan stops which have marked the trade routes between East and West for milleniums. A wall enclosed a square courtyard where the horses and donkeys lodged. Along the high wall were stalls or small rooms, most of them without either furniture, windows or doors.

Frank sought out the best room available—one with a mud floor covered with a fresh straw matting—and paid for a night's lodging. The hour was late and they were both bone-weary. They ate a little food from their lunch basket, and Frank put up their traveling cots. Florence watched her husband with a feeling of gratitude and admiration. He had thought of everything. What if they hadn't had the cots and had to sleep right down on the *haseer* with the bugs.

"Welcome to Persia, sweetheart!" Frank cheerfully pushed the food box under his cot.

Just then they heard a commotion in their open doorway, and half a dozen rough, dark-browed men strode in. Florence had started up in alarm. Frank greeted them in their own language, "*Salaam Aleykum!* [Peace be with you!]."

The men made themselves at home on the floor, and Frank kept a smooth conversation flowing with them. Florence eyed their guns—not a man was unarmed—and their baggy clothes, which might conceal—who knew how many more—weapons. They looked like bandits, every one. Frank, however, was opening his Bible. Turning every encounter into a missionary opportunity was instinctive with him. He read 1 Corinthians 13 to the men in their own language.

"I'm reading the love chapter," Frank whispered to Florence. In this peculiar and threatening situation the more said about love the better, she felt. Then Frank offered prayer.

Getting up briskly he turned to the men, "*Khoda Hafez* [God keep you]." No one moved.

"We're staying all night with you," one of them said with assurance.

"Have all of them in the room all night?" Florence asked in

a whisper to Frank. "Surely not!"

"Why must you stay here all night?" Frank inquired.

"Why, to protect you, *Agha* of course!" they chorused.

"But we'll be quite all right." Frank tried edging a couple of them toward the door. "I assure you, we'll—"

"Oh, no *Agha*." The chief spokesman leaned over confidentially to relate his dreadful tale. "Do you know that only last night a stranger occupied this very room? And after he was asleep and all things were quiet, thieves came and robbed him of all his goods? They even carried away the rug upon which he was sleeping."

Frank turned to his trembling bride. "I'm sorry, Floss. We can't get rid of them. It would be dangerous to press the matter. But it will be all right. We won't be in danger during the night."

So the entire party bedded down for the night, the men lying across the doorway and along the walls. Frank and Florence lay down on their cots. In the dark Florence reached out for Frank's comforting hand. He squeezed hers and whispered, "Don't worry, dear one. Truly, it'll be all right."

But Florence couldn't sleep. She listened to the heavy breathing all around her in the close, cramped quarters of the mud-walled stall. Occasionally she heard a snort or a grunt nearby. How many other brides had nights like this on their honeymoon trip? And then she had to smile to herself in the dark at the incongruity of it all.

But it turned out to be as Frank promised. They got up at dawn, safe and untroubled. Their "guards" had seen to it that no tragedy had befallen the innocent foreigners during the night. Frank, of course, knew what would come next. They each wanted their *bakhshesh* for the services they had rendered. This could well be the most difficult part of the encounter.

They were not satisfied with Frank's initial donation, and the discussion heated up among them. After all, had they not risked life and limb for the sake of the Americans? Frank added more money, and at last the matter was amicably settled. Florence noted unhappily that their private guard service had really cost them quite a substantial sum. If she could have seen ahead, however, she would have realized that this was neither the first nor the last time she would spend the night in a Persian *caravansary* under the protection of "special guards".

Four days and three *caravansary* nights later, the Osters arrived in Urmia. The journey from Europe had taken three months. For Frank this was a homecoming, for he had already spent two years in this ancient city west of Lake Urmia. It traced itself back to the empire of the Medes and was supposed by many to be the birthplace of Zoroaster, the founder of Persia's ancient "fire religion." Frank had come to feel much at home here in Urmia, and pointed out places of interest to Florence along the way.

Just at the edge of the city the carriage driver began to act very strangely. Fearful sounds gurgled up from his throat, and his body began to weave back and forth in his seat. He rolled his eyes in a most frightening manner. "What's he clowning around for?" Frank started up. "Hey, you—"

"No, wait! Frank, he's having a fit, I think. Help him," Florence cried. Frank leaped up to grab the reins and stop the horses. At the same moment Florence and Hussein, one of the little helper boys who invariably accompanied drivers on long trips, caught the convulsed body of the driver as he reeled forward, almost falling under the horses' hooves.

They managed to get him stretched out on the ground, where his epileptic seizure finally exhausted itself. Frank and Florence were primarily concerned that he should not injure himself. Little Hussein envisioned yet another dire possibility, however, and he hurriedly found a stick and drew a line all the way around the prostrate form of his master so that the Evil Eye couldn't affect him.

When the driver had partially recovered, they managed to get him into the seat beside Florence. His glazed eyes and limp body still testified to the violence of the seizure, and she had to hang onto him to prevent his falling out of the carriage onto the street.

Attended by the faithful Hussein, Frank got up into the driver's seat and drove the rest of the way into the city. Passersby seemed to be highly entertained by the view of the Christian missionary, high in the driver's perch, bringing his new wife into Urmia while she held the swaying, befuddled driver on the seat behind. It was almost a grotesque kind of "triumphal arrival," for some bystanders recognized Frank Oster and greeted him. They saw that he was, indeed, bringing his bride home to Persia in style.

Maragha Housekeeping

When Frank had concluded his affairs in Urmia, the Osters, with the approval of the European Division, moved to Maragha on the eastern side of the lake. It was fifty miles south of Tabriz, as the vultures flew. No missionaries had ever lived in this city before.

As their carriage approached the outskirts, Frank asked the driver to stop. "Floss, we face a great responsibility for God here. Let's ask Him right now for His help. I feel we're going to need it in a very particular way."

Hand in hand they got down; walked over the roadside embankment to a large, sheltering rock; and knelt down behind it. "Dear Father, go before us and prepare the way," Frank prayed. "Be to us a Rock of strength, and impress the people of this city to receive us with kindness so that we may, through Thy grace, win them for Thy kingdom."

Florence's eyes grew misty as they turned back to their waiting phaeton. They were so very much alone. And yet not really alone, for they had just requested help from the greatest Source of wisdom in the universe—and with immediate results. At least, so it seemed.

As they approached the city gate, they saw someone coming out toward them. It was the Armenian *keshish* (priest). "I heard you were coming," the priest said gravely. "And I come to welcome you to our city, on behalf of the 300 Armenian Christian families here." He and Frank talked together for several minutes before the carriage moved on.

"Before they call, I will answer," Florence breathed in astonishment.

"And while they are yet speaking, I will hear," Frank finished the verse (Isaiah 65:24). "God did it again!"

In Maragha they found Dr. Joel. An Assyrian who had studied medicine in the United States, he was the only person in town besides themselves who could speak English. This discovery was a happy one on both sides. Help in a time of real need for the newcomers, on one hand, and a chance for the doctor to revive his long-dormant English, on the other. He became their first friend, and a true one.

He helped them find a house to rent from an Armenian family. Most of the Persians lived in one-room mud huts with a hole in the roof to let the smoke from their fires escape. So this, by local standards, turned out to be a very good house. High mud walls protected it on all sides. The rooms on the first floor would be adequate for holding meetings, and above them were two other rooms. One would be a bedroom and the other a living-dining room. In the rear of the latter Frank made a small kitchen. Even remnants of whitewash were to be found here and there. A few little windows opened out toward their pitiful little scrap of a yard.

Florence cleaned. At first she wondered how she would fare trying to "clean" mud floors and walls, but she discovered that noticeable improvements were possible.

Frank, meanwhile, made some architectural changes. As the weather was beginning to get warmer, he decided to cut a small window in the wide mud wall at the back. The need for some cross-ventilation had become quite evident. "There!" he said as he dusted off his hands. "It's simple to make a window."

A pleasant whisper of a breeze now stirred across the house. "And it's much lighter too," Florence added. "That will be very nice. In the morning I'll find another sheet to use for a curtain."

Early the next morning, however, they became conscious that a certain gloom had settled over the place again. "Why, Frank, look!" Florence pointed in amazement. "Our new window! It's gone!"

And sure enough, it had been covered with fresh mud and plastered shut. Curiosity contended with disappointment in their minds. What in the world had happened? "I'll go and see that neighbor whose yard adjoins our back wall." Frank headed down the steps.

In a few minutes he was back. "Floss, we committed a great error in opening the window. It's against Persian law to have a window facing a neighbor's yard."

"It is?" Florence was incredulous.

"Yes. He said he could have had me arrested, but since I didn't know any better, he just took care of it himself."

"But why?" Florence couldn't imagine how many times she had asked that question since they left western Europe.

"Well, of course, you know I might look through that window and see his women." They both laughed at the picture of Frank spending his hours at the window trying to steal a glimpse of the beauties of his neighbor's harem. "So naturally they had to get it closed up—and quickly too."

Several days later, however, Frank undertook some other major alterations. "I've hit my head on this door for the last time," he declared, as he began cutting away above the doorway between their two private rooms. The improvement of being able to walk from one room to the other without bending low at the entrance was ridiculously pleasing to both of them.

The stairs going up to the second floor presented problems too. They were made of mud, and the steps varied in height from six to eighteen inches. No matter how you tried to memorize the pattern of sizes, every ascent and descent became a frustration—like trying to do a steady four-beat march to the swaying tune of a three-beat waltz.

"I suppose our neighbors won't mind if I make some changes in *here*," Frank muttered, as he started tearing out the entire stairway. He found some lumber which he cut by hand. Making each step just eight inches high, he constructed a very convenient and substantial staircase.

News quickly spread that the American had built a wooden staircase in his house. Such a thing had never been heard of before, and the people began coming from all over town to see the wonderful stairs. "It flows down, beautiful just like a river," said one. "It's all so even, just like tiles," exclaimed another. While impressions varied from one sightseer to another, all agreed that it was the most remarkable piece of construction they had ever seen.

In many ways Frank was the ideal missionary, putting in long hours in his ministry and also being a real handyman at home. His furniture—precision-made—had quality too: a beautiful, large, hardwood bookcase; a lovely writing desk with four drawers, pigeonholes, and a bookshelf; and a stool for the organ. That marvelous organ! It was the first ever to come to Maragha. Both Frank and Florence enjoyed playing and singing. Then came a folding ironing board and a wardrobe. And above all, the screen door made with precious screening brought all the way from Germany. Although her neighbors may not have valued this item as highly as some of her other possessions, for Florence, having a kitchen free from flies and other pests was a treasure beyond reckoning. As far as she was concerned, it would have been worth it to have carried the screen all the way from Massachusetts, if need be.

The Osters had been fortunate in finding a good bed in Urmia. When Florence realized that practically everyone in Persia slept on the floor and used their blanket rolls as sofas during the day, she was amazed that they had even found a bed for sale anywhere in the country. The total furnishings in Persian homes seemed to be blankets, beautiful rugs, and rifles. Carpets were one thing that the Osters couldn't afford immediately—other things stood higher on their list of priorities. Florence indulged herself once in a while, however, in a dream of the day when she might be able to have one. Meantime, floors had to be spread with straw and covered with tightly stretched burlap nailed into the hard mud.

Keeping warm during the long winter evenings was a problem to be solved in various ways. Families often gathered with their neighbors and visitors around a low table under which was placed a bowl of glowing coals. Then quilts were spread over the low table and the laps of the people sitting around the table. Whiling away the evening exchanging news and telling tales constituted the chief entertainment. Perhaps the custom contributed to the fact that the Persians have long been avid storytellers. For the rest of the night, then, the family would sleep here with their feet near the pot of coals in the center and their heads poking out from the edges of the quilts like the spokes of a wheel.

A few of the more enterprising families made stoves of sheet iron, sort of airtight heaters. But probably no more than a dozen of these crude heaters existed among Maragha's 60,000 inhabitants. Florence's cookstove from Germany was the first of its kind in the town. It opened up possibilities in cooking which no woman in Maragha had ever considered before. The stove had cost a great deal to get all the way to Maragha, what with both Russian and Persian duties, plus transportation costs, but not a day passed that Florence didn't feel a special depth of gratitude for it.

Holes in the ground heated with hot stones were the traditional kind of Persian oven. What came out of them was unique and edible in its own way. Florence soon learned to join Frank in eating *lavash,* the local Persian bread, which was about the shape and thickness of a large oval face towel. Although she had a few reservations about certain stages of its production, she had to set them aside, for variety in food was not so great that one could afford to reject the staple item in the national diet.

The preparation of the dough and the baking of the *lavash* occupied a crew of bakers for two days. First, the connoisseur of the group selected the flour in the bazaar by means of the spittle test. That is, a sample of flour was placed in the palm of the hand, spat upon, mixed into a little dough, and then carefully examined for gluten content.

On mixing day the head baker thoroughly mixed the high-gluten flour, salt, and sour dough in a huge trough. He turned the dough out onto a large sheet on the hard, smooth earth and placed another sheet on top of it. At this point work turned into play. The first person jumping on the kneading floor earned the privilege of eating the first pieces of bread to come out of the oven. Friends and neighbors joyously joined the bakers, and with bare feet they all danced on the dough to the age-old eastern rhythms beaten out by a tambourine player. This social event ended when the chief baker announced that sufficient kneading had been done, and the upper sheet was removed. The lump of dough spent the night back in the trough, left to rise until the next morning.

At dawn on baking day the large subterranean oven was loaded with *yapmah* (sun-dried patties of dung). They were ignited and burned slowly until the smoke disappeared. Left to glow and heat, the *yapmah* brought the oven to the right temperature. Four women formed an assembly line, beginning at the dough trough and ending at the oven. The first formed the dough into a baseball-size lump and the second rolled it out with a long thin rolling pin called a *torlama*. The third skillfully tossed the sheet of dough until it expanded to about two feet in diameter and then laid it on a padded board. The fourth slapped it down onto the smooth, hot rounded side of the oven. Watching for just the right color and texture, she always knew when the *lavash* was thoroughly baked.

The crisp, dry sheets of *lavash* stacked almost to the ceiling made a supply that would last for many weeks. Each evening the women sprinkled a few sheets of it with water, and the next day the moist bread was ready to eat.

Frank had told Florence that the Persians used neither dishes nor silverware, so she was thankful for what she had brought from Germany. The Persian people ate from one common earthen dish using their fingers or a piece of their bread. Florence admired the dainty way they could eat with their *lavash* without soiling their fingers at all.

Although Florence enjoyed watching the processes of making the *lavash* and the taste of the crispy pieces, by early 1914 she longed to make some of her own kind of bread. True, they had plenty of eggs and potatoes, but her mind kept dwelling on cornflakes, oatmeal, and mush. When the craving for some tidbits from home became quite overwhelming, she finally gave in and wrote to Vandella, "Please send me some kind of breakfast food just to see if it will come through without duty. There is absolutely nothing like that here. We have plenty—but I get *tired* of it."

It took four months, but the package came through duty-free and still intact. Frank and Florence rejoiced over their treasures—herb tea, malted milk, cocoa, Cream of Wheat, and so forth. They looked at the things, admired them, and finally, in careful allotments, ate them. Above all, there was yeast, and Florence, with a little fanfare, brought out her first western loaf of bread to supplement the *lavash*. Quite enraptured with it, Frank declared it to be the best bread he'd ever eaten—anytime, anyplace.

Occasionally the Osters purchased white flour, but it's price really lay beyond the scope of their small income. The flour had to be used sparingly—for a little gravy or, once in a very great while, a cake. Since raisins were cheap, Florence made a fine art of baking English raisin scones (buns). Poverty, not luxury, stimulates creativity, and despite all the culinary problems to which she had to find solutions, Florence performed some quite remarkable feats.

"What've we got today, Floss?" Frank eyed the table hopefully, pulled up his chair and lifted the lid off one dish. "Umm. Mushrooms! And lettuce! So, our 'market garden' finally produced, eh?"

"Well, not robustly, perhaps," Florence replied with modesty. "But I think it's quite good, all things considered."

The "garden" planted in the very poor soil of their tiny, six-by-ten foot yard was a matter of constant, loving concern. They had brought the seeds from Germany. The lettuce had done fairly well, and they could eat it with carefree relish, knowing that it hadn't been nurtured in night soil (human fertilizer). A couple of cauliflower heads had attained maturity, along with a few carrots. The peas made a poor showing, but the dozen pods they harvested at least reminded them that such things as peas still grew in the world. A border of sweet peas and nasturtiums lent the garden a bold, gay dash of color.

Frank helped himself liberally to the steaming casserole of scalloped potatoes. An amazing number of good things can be done with the lowly potato, and Florence had discovered most of them. "I've got a surprise for dessert," she warned.

When she set his bowl of shortcake before him, Frank was properly astonished. "How did you manage *this*?"

"It's made out of dried *holoo* (peaches). But you're supposed to think of strawberry shortcake while you eat it. That's what the folks back home are having now, you know. I think this tastes pretty good with the cream. And," she added, "the cream *is* genuine."

Frank agreed that it was a quite reasonable facsimile of strawberry shortcake. "And since we're being so festive today," he suggested, "why don't you bring out some of those cherries I found in the bazaar last night?"

When Florence returned with the bowl of cherries, she looked at them meditatively. "You know, Frank, I believe this is the first fresh fruit we've had since we arrived here." She set the bowl down on the table. "I suppose we oughtn't to be eating all our goodies at one meal," she said as she sat down opposite him.

Frank reached across the table and laid his hand over hers. "I think we ought to be celebrating the fact that we've both learned to live so well in Persia—and to do it with contentment and joy."

One Woman's World

Frank stood looking through the window at their tiny garden, with a frown of distaste. The brave little rows of lettuce and carrots seemed to give him no joy this time. "Floss," he called.

Florence came out of the kitchen, dish towel in hand.

"Floss, don't you think we've looked at these bed sheets hanging on our windows long enough? Let's go to town and see if we can find some material for curtains."

"Wonderful! Oh, marvelous." Florence was already untying her apron, for she had no wish to thwart such a good impulse. "I was just hoping you'd suggest something like that."

In another moment she came out of the bedroom, adjusting her hat. "I've been wanting to get out of the house for ages too. Let's walk to town this time," she urged.

Winter had finally retreated, and the sun generated a lot of heat. So much so, that they chose to walk along in the shade of the high mud walls as they made their way to the bazaar. They noticed that a surprising number of people seemed to have arrived at the bazaar right along with them, intent on their shopping, they went on without taking much note of the heavy flow of traffic into the marketplace.

Turning into the yardage shop, they quickly became engrossed in turning over bolts of cloth and discussing the virtues of one against another. Suddenly they became aware of a great mob gathered outside the store. The pressure and very weight of their presence could be felt, as well as seen. When the crowd began pressing into the shop, Frank and Florence really became alarmed.

To her horror Florence realized that the crowd was made up entirely of men—old, young, and the full range in between. Moreover, they all gazed intently—at *her!* She had come out without her veil! How could the sunny spring weather have made her so careless?

The shopkeeper's feeble remonstrances had little effect on the singleminded mob that kept pouring in. Perhaps he too was a little mesmerized. Frank, however, laid a firm hand on the merchant's shoulder. "Look, if the whole town is going to gather here, we'll have to leave."

Fearful that he would lose a sale, the old man began pushing the human tide back into the street. "My customers! Outside, outside, all of you. Be gone!"

Frank and Florence now selected their curtain fabric without further deliberation and hastily sought the privacy of a phaeton to take them home. "Well, that's the first, last and only time I'm going to town without my veil!" Florence promised.

"A good idea," Frank agreed. "At least until such a time as Persian customs begin to catch up with the twentieth century."

And Florence kept her word, although she regarded her *chador* (veil) with loathing. The huge black sheet hung to the floor, both front and back, and was topped with a yard of linen perforated with two minute holes for the eyes. Two large bags for the feet and legs completed the costume, and a woman on the street would be wholly unrecognizable, even to her own husband. Florence always remembered her first glimpse of the veiled Persian women in Tiflis. She wondered again when their freedom would come. Meanwhile, on this one sensitive point, she would have to be content to be one of them.

Upon arrival at home, Florence immediately set about the business of measuring the windows again and making up the new curtains. Frank, however, threw himself on the bed. "I'm tired, Floss. I'll just rest a bit."

That night he felt too tired to bother getting up for supper. And the next morning, though he did get out of bed, he still seemed too tired to accomplish anything. "I can't understand it. I haven't exerted myself in any extra way," he sighed.

Florence couldn't understand it either—this wasn't at all like Frank. Then, after three days, the fever struck. Together they searched the pages of *The Practical Guide to Health,* and both agreed that he must have typhoid. His temperature held at 103°, and Dr. Joel came morning and evening to administer a little medicine. But that didn't make much difference.

Florence ministered to him round the clock, bathing him with cool sponges, holding an ice bag to his head and, at times, his heart. For the first few days she gave him only raisin juice and *doogh,* a local drink made of water, yogurt and salt. Then she tried barley water.

Just when she had exhausted all her dietary recources for the sick room, another food parcel came from Vandella. The gruel which Florence made from the cereals and the malted milk seemed to be just the right thing—partly, perhaps, because they were so rare. At any rate they interested the patient, and that was good.

Although this was the Osters' first major bout with illness, it would be neither the last nor the worst. But this time, with youth and vigorous health on his side and with a totally dedicated nurse, Frank made a rapid and complete recovery.

Elsewhere the epidemic raged on. A young girl in a neighboring house became ill. Frank and Florence heard about it in the evening, and they awoke the next morning to the sounds of wailing all through the district. According to custom, the child was buried almost immediately, and then preparations began for several days of ceremonial mourning. An immense kettle of meat and bitter herbs was set out to be served, with tea, to sympathizing guests.

The Osters went to pay their respects. The host ushered Frank into the men's mourning room, and servants led Florence along to the women's room at the back. There she joined the circle of women sitting on the floor and listened to the chief hired mourner enumerating the good deeds of the little girl. Her recitation was punctuated intermittently, and at unexpected moments, with her howling and wailing. Every time the girl's name was mentioned, the mourners, the family, and the friends, with tears coursing down their cheeks, howled so loudly that they could be heard blocks away.

Then all at once everyone stopped crying, and a servant went around with water and a towel so all could wash their hands and faces. During this intermission tea was served, and the guests talked and chatted amiably with one another. This performance was repeated for each new crowd of visitors, with the hired mourners staying to weep and wail with each group.

"Frank," Florence said as they walked home together, "I feel so truly sorry about the loss of the little girl. The tears couldn't *all* have been hired, I'm sure."

"They weren't. But those poor, ignorant people have no hope—none," Frank replied. "Oh, the message we have is so important for them—but it's such a slow process. If only we could give them what they need most—now, tonight!"

"Just *no* way to hurry it, though," Florence replied. "But God still has His time clock, remember?" It was Florence's turn to encourage Frank. "Persia's somehow in His plan, and here we are for Him to use."

Some weeks later Florence went visiting with Mrs. Joel and gleaned further insights into the private life of Persia. Together they called on four wealthy Moslem ladies. Florence never passed up an opportunity to visit the women or to encourage them to visit her.

This time the graciousness of the home charmed Florence. Gorgeous flower gardens lay under the shade of great trees, watered by fountains. Beauty on every side—who couldn't be happy here? Well, she soon discovered who wasn't happy there—the women who lived in this paradise: a mother, a daughter, and two daughters-in-law. Driven by loneliness and misery, they opened their sorrowful hearts that afternoon to their visitors.

They were separated from even their own husbands, who lived in other apartments outside the high mud walls of their lovely prison. No other man, of course, would dare set foot inside the ladies' quarters.

"A few months ago while I was very ill," the mother moaned, "my husband deserted me and married three other women."

To this tale one of the younger women added an even more fantastic story. "My father, who used to be the *mullah* (religious chief) here in Maragha, took forty *sughehs* [concubines] and fifty divorced women."

"You mean he was married to ninety women at one time?" Florence exclaimed.

"Yes. But of course each one was confined to her own yard; so that saved him some trouble. Finally he got tired of all of them, divorced them and went to Tabriz. He's married to four other women and living with them there now."

Florence looked from one woman to another—beautiful, intelligent women with so much to offer. But they were trapped in a centuries-old system. Amid their own lovely gardens, they were themselves as withered, starved plants.

"You foreigners have such good husbands," one of the young women sighed. "We have observed it. They're very good to you."

"Yes," Florence replied, "we're thankful for our good husbands. I thank God every day for mine. But let me tell you something. All of God's faithful children can find a truly happy home in heaven." Like Frank, she had learned to turn every conversation so that it pointed upward. "For all those who have not had happiness here, I think there must be a special reward—an extra amount of love just for them."

Summer heat brought almost as many problems as had the cold of winter. So Frank and Florence took up what seemed to be a very sensible Persian custom. Like all of their neighbors, they escaped the hot night air indoors and slept on the flat mud roof of their home. Frank constructed a canvas lean-to over their cots to keep off the rain, and inside the shelter he made a mosquito-net tent with netting brought from Germany.

Florence sometimes wondered if there could be *any* domestic need which Frank had not foreseen in Germany. While they had been shopping there, Florence had occasionally wondered about the need of some of the purchases. Frank, however, had pursued the buying with such conviction that she had questioned nothing. So now, while their neighbors spread a rug and rolled themselves up in quilts to keep off the insects, the Osters slept, cool and secure, in their net tent. They were, to be sure, the aristocrats among all the roof-sleepers in Maragha.

One household event in which Florence chose not to join her Maragha neighbors was washday at the river. Despite the fact that it was a regular social gathering place, the possibility of losing pieces of clothing threatened continually. Therefore, Narrine was hired. She did the washing and sweeping, but on her own terms. Refusing to use Florence's washboard, she did the entire wash while squatting on the ground beside the shallow laundry tub. She also washed the dishes squatting on the floor.

To Florence all of this seemed unnecessarily difficult, but squatting seemed to be the approved posture for a surprising number of household chores, including sawing and planing boards while sitting on them. She had even seen women squatting while they chopped wood. Florence was willing, however, to relinquish some of her opinions and give in to the customs of the land. She needed household help, and, as missionary wives everywhere learn to do, she became willing to make concessions so that household chores could be accomplished more or less efficiently.

On the point of drinking-water, however, Florence was adamant. The water supply came from the *ab-ambar* (cistern) under the house. Its water level was maintained by the periodic flooding of the ditches along the roadside. With the water came dead cats, hens, and all sorts of debris—to join the resident frogs. The Osters kept a rain barrel outside. All water used for drinking or food preparation had to be boiled—that was a regulation as firm as the famous "laws of the Medes and Persians."

Florence needed help that summer, and she would need more help come December. Florence and Frank expected their first child to arrive before Christmas. Letters home now became preoccupied with such things as outing flannel and tips on baby care. Vandella's nursing experience established her as a long-distance counselor while Florence prepared for this exciting new event. An order went off to Montgomery Ward's in mid-July for a layette, so that the newcomer would be well provided for upon arrival.

"Frank, do you suppose that Mrs. Joel could come here to help me when the baby comes?" Florence asked.

"I hardly think so. She's a very busy person here in the city," Frank replied. "Perhaps we could arrange for Sister Staubert from Tabriz to come down and spend a couple of weeks with us. Since she's from Germany, we could trust her and her ways of doing things, I'm sure."

"No," Florence objected. "That would be expecting too much for her to come all the way from Tabriz. It's too far. I've got a better idea." Florence had long since learned to have complete confidence in Frank's judgment and ability. "I think you will make a better nurse than anyone else. Narrine can take more responsibility with the housework, and we'll get along fine. I've been following all the prenatal-care suggestions from Vandella very carefully, you know."

"All?" Frank queried. "How about the exercise?"

"Well, that's a point," Florence had to admit. "Putting on that wretched long veil discourages me from taking long walks, I know. I'm afraid I'll stumble over it and fall down."

"But it seems to me that that was a rather important part of Vandella's instructions." Frank pressed the issue.

"It was. But I promise to get my exercise here at home." Florence felt optimistic about the future. Hadn't God given them this baby? And He knew the situation.

"Good. Then I'll accept my appointment as head nurse," Frank agreed. "And fortunately by December the weather will be cooler. That means that the flies, mosquitoes, and fleas will be dormant."

On the international scene chaos reigned that fall. On the Osters' domestic front time passed uneventfully. Then at midnight on the 28th day of November Frank had his first call to duty. "Frank!" Florence whispered in his ear. "The pains have started!" He leaped out of bed with such alacrity that Florence had to laugh.

"We'll move the bed into the living room," he said. "You'll be more comfortable there and we'll have more room."

The baby, however, had only put them on the alert and apparently had no further plans for that night. Nor the next day either, for that matter. Florence went about her household chores that day as usual.

Then, at two o'clock the next night, December 1, little Winona Lucille arrived. Dr. Joel offered Florence some chloroform in a glass to inhale from time to time. Since Persian women will never see a male doctor, his experience in obstetrics had been limited. It took him what seemed hours to make the six stitches necessary for the repair work. He spent most of the time hunting for broken needles. To Florence, the pain was excruciating, but in another way it hurt Frank still more. He had to help the doctor, and the sweat stood in great drops on his face. Finally, he insisted that Florence be given more chloroform. The doctor had to go home to get some more.

After it was all over and she was awake again, Frank said, "Floss, I think we need to pray especially that you'll be all right now. The doctor's procedures were certainly not sterile. He used an old jar of vaseline, and when I asked him how long it had been open, he said he guessed about a year. And his fingernails were very dirty too." So, very simply, the young missionaries prayed about it—that God would tend to the germs and Florence would be spared further complications or infection. And she was.

The first time the baby needed her diaper changed, Florence asked Narrine to tend to her. In one decisive motion the woman stripped the baby, band-dressing and all, and held her in one hand over a pan, dousing her with water—all before Florence could recover from her surprise and say a word. Needless to day, from then on Frank himself became sole nurse for the baby until Florence was able to take over the work.

Winona brought a new kind of brightness into their home—a kind that no opening of any window in a mud wall could match. Loved and cared for like a small princess, she slept and grew and made her way deep into the hearts of her parents.

But certainly Winona's wardrobe had nothing very royal about it. The order from Montgomery Ward's had never arrived—no, not even in six months. Her one new nightgown came from her Aunt Vandella, and it suffered a sad, untimely end. The first time Florence washed it and hung it on the clothesline, someone stole it! Florence could have wept.

But now, skilled in the art of making-do, she took one of her own old nightgowns and made three for the baby. Her sewing machine became more precious than ever before. "It's well worth the forty dollars it cost to bring it into the country," she told Frank. "It's been worth that much already, with just the baby's things alone."

Now with a cozy little family of three and established missionary interests, everything seemed to fall into place. Frank and Florence not only enjoyed their work, but they enjoyed Winona with sheer delight. Florence would study the tiny pink face and insist that she looked like Frank. He would hold her up to the lamplight and declare that she would someday be as lovely as her mother.

Meanwhile, the shadows of war which fell across the world in late 1914 steadily lengthened. There was no way that Frank and Florence could know that before the next Christmas the shadows would darken their path, and that disaster would break over their own heads.

Living With Terror

Frank and Florence each created a "missionary niche" for themselves in Maragha. Frank conducted meetings and held Bible studies in the downstairs parlor. The people, as was their custom, sat on the floor. The organ proved to be a prime attraction, as Florence guessed it would be.

From the first moment she arrived in Persia, Florence recognized that she had to learn the language, and she seized every opportunity to improve her proficiency. The Turkish language was the most used in that area. Therefore, she used the Bible as her Turkish textbook. She sometimes taught her Moslem teacher the meaning of the texts, while he taught her the mechanics of the language. Upon her arrival in Maragha Florence gathered a group of neighbor girls to teach them English, which they were eager enough to learn. Florence's Turkish improved rapidly also, and after a time a few of the girls began to keep the Sabbath. All of which proved that lessons other than those of language had been taught and learned.

Members of the group at Frank's meetings also began keeping the Sabbath, one by one. Mirza Shmuel (Samuel) and his wife Javaher came while they were vacationing in Maragha. They were well-educated Christian Jews, and served in the Lutheran Mission in Sāūjbulāgh (now Mahābād) where Shmuel worked as translator and interpreter.

His fascination with Seventh-day Adventism led him through a series of thrilling discoveries. "Marvelous!" he exclaimed to Frank. "So that means I can be a Christian and still keep the Sabbath!" Suddenly everything in his loyal Jewish soul seemed reconciled. His introduction to Ellen White and her writings was equally enthusiastic. "A prophetess!" he cried. "More revelation to guide us!" When the Osters suggested they eat, Shmuel insisted, "No! No! we can eat later—let us learn more now." So, scarcely stopping to sleep or eat, Shmuel studied daily with Frank.

When his vacation time was over, he came to say good-bye. "I will return again to Maragha with my family, Oster *Kardash* [Brother Oster]." Shmuel's intense handshake bespoke his earnest, sincere character. "When my wife has delivered her child, we will return. We must learn more and then we will be baptized again—to become Seventh-day Adventists."

Encounters with people like Mirza Shmuel shone like bright stars of pure joy in the lives of Frank and Florence. So much of the time their work seemed to be halted by a vast, impenetrable barrier. Sometimes the obstacles oppressed them like an unseen shadow, for they were two lone Christians face to face with the mighty forces of Islam. And then when someone like Shmuel came along, they not only studied with him but daily held him up, a precious trophy, before God. And new courage would flow through them like a vitalizing river of strength.

About ten days after Mirza Shmuel and Javaher had returned to Sāūjbulāgh, Frank came home one afternoon, his face ashen. Florence rushed to him as a flood of fear welled up in her. "Frank, are you sick?"

"No— Well, yes." He sat down heavily.

"What's wrong. Oh, tell me!" Florence could read disaster all over his face, and her mind groped for a cause.

"Floss, it's Shmuel."

"Shmuel?" Florence's mind raced on, from one frantic possibility to another. "What happened to him?"

"He's dead." Frank spoke with hopeless finality. "Murdered."

Florence's heart tightened into a knot. "Dead!" The moment her mind comprehended this fearful fact, it leaped to another thought. "Poor, poor Javaher, and her baby,—. What happened to it?"

"It was delivered very soon after Shmuel died."

"What happened, Frank? How could such a fine man have enemies who would—"

"It's the Kurds, again," Frank replied slowly. "With the Kurds you don't need enemies. There's no reason or logic to it. A Kurd had simply become angry with one of the foreigners at the Lutheran mission, and he vowed to kill the next person who came out of the compound gate. And that person was Shmuel."

For a moment Frank and Florence sat in silence while the weight of the news adjusted and arranged itself in their minds. "The Kurds plundered and destroyed everything," Frank added. "Javaher is left with nothing, I hear."

"Then let's send for her," Florence urged. "We must help her until she can make her own way. Four children and alone! Oh, poor, dear Javaher!"

And so the Osters took in the widow and all her children. Florence wrote to Vandella to see if someone at home might be interested in helping the children. Twelve-year-old Lazarus had learned Turkish well and was rapidly picking up English too. Javaher proved herself worthy of their confidence, and despite her desperate need she refused to accept work on Sabbath.

The death of Mr. Shmuel proved to be a harbinger of things to come. The Kurds—a fierce, warlike, and generally nomadic tribe—lived in the Zagros Mountains between Persia, Turkey, and what is now Iraq. Of sturdy, strong-featured Aryan stock, they were, nonetheless, devoted Moslems. Armed to the teeth with knives and guns, clad in loose, flowing *ammameh* (turbans) and baggy trousers with colorful sashes, the wild Kurds made a romantic but terrible spectacle.

No group in the entire Middle East—perhaps in the world—has had a greater capacity for plunder and carnage. With their rifles and daggers and swift, surefooted ponies, the hordes swept down out of the hills. No wagons, no heavy artillery, nothing to hinder their speed. Usually they killed the men and old people and kidnapped the girls and young women. Carrying their loot to a safe distance, they would store it in a cache and return again.

These fierce marauders, however, are not entirely to be blamed for their predatory way of life. They had been harried by the lowland peoples as far back as the time of the Assyrian Empire and of necessity have been driven to live in the mountains with their sheep and goats. One passionte desire still burns within many of them even to the present day—to realize a free and independent Kurdistan. And death has always seemed a perfectly reasonable price to pay in such a cause.

Now, as the war warmed up toward the end of 1914, Turkey, a member of the Central Powers, saw in the Kurds a weapon to be used against the Russians occupying Azerbaijan, the northwest province of Persia. Led by a few Turkish soldiers, the Kurds were eager to fight. Laying waste the countryside had, after all, been their daily bread for thousands of years.

A mixture of Moslems, Jews, and Christians (Syrian and Armenian) lived on the great plain of Urmia (the well-watered place). It was dotted with villages and a veritable forest of vineyards and orchards. Russian presence in the area had established a degree of peace and order. Free from Moslem persecution, Christians had built houses, gained high levels of education, and had come to enjoy a prosperity that had made the Moslems bitter. The latter, however, concealed their jealousy and bided their time.

This "golden age" was of short duration, and now the Russian garrisons stationed in Azerbaijan were ordered south to fight the oncoming Kurds.

From the onset of the war, the Christians in Persia had been filled with fear and evil forebodings—and not without reason. As their Moslem neighbors cleaned their old rifles and sharpened their rusty swords in preparation for the time when the Russians should be driven out, apprehensive Christians began to disappear, fleeing north to places unknown.

Yet now, as the Russian troops passed through Maragha, they kept assuring the few remaining Christians not to worry. It would only be a matter of an engagement or two, and they would drive the Kurds back into the mountains. Still, Frank and Florence watched developments with mounting concern.

Florence was caring for baby Winona, now just three weeks old, when Frank arrived home one day at mid-morning. "Floss, I'm worried. I don't know what we should do." He stamped the snow off his boots, pulled off his gloves, and rubbed his hands briskly.

"Are there still many Russians in town?" Florence asked.

"Quite a few. But I heard that the Kurds have actually destroyed their ammunition dump to the south and have cut off their supply route. That's why they all came back up here to Maragha." Frank frowned. "And they've been telling us that they came back to defend Maragha better."

"You know, Frank, the city's been full of Christians fleeing north," Florence said. "You remember what Heghena told us just a couple of days ago—how the Kurds kill." Florence picked up Winona and held her close. "She said she saw them cut children in two and throw them into the icy river."

"We've prayed for God's protection," Frank paced the small room, hands behind his back. "We've waited in faith— But now—"

Florence could remember the stories their friend had told all too clearly. "And Heghena escaped only by swimming the river, you know. She begged us to flee north without further delay."

"I know. And I've discovered another odd thing this morning. The Russians keep marching out to the north gate of town, supposedly to do guard duty. But none of them ever come back." Frank paused in his pacing and put his arm around Florence. "Dear one, I think you'd better prepare some things for the baby and for us. It may be that we'll have to leave on short notice. Pray that we'll somehow be led to do the right thing today."

Florence watched as Frank left to investigate further clues. What *was* going on in Maragha? And now, to leave their little home? In such weather, on such a mission, and with a three-week-old baby! Florence's head swam, and she had to sit down to steady herself. "Lord, give us strength," she murmured. Then she began to prepare—for what? Who could tell?

Determined to know the truth, Frank sought out the Russian commandant. The military post was surrounded by an agitated crowd. The Kurds! Where are they? Will they attack our city? How shall we defend ourselves? Anxiety pervaded the very air, but the officer assured them all, in Russian, *"Nyet, karasho!* [No, all is well!]" The people murmured in confusion, but the commander could speak only Russian, not Turkish.

Frank had been hearing this propaganda for several days and was beginning to believe it less and less. Then suddenly, the officer turned to Frank and announced in plain, clear English, "We leave tonight at midnight." So, it was out! The Russians *were* abandoning Maragha, and doing it that very night. What would happen next?

Now the decision became clear. This would be their last chance to escape. Frank hurried off in search of a horse to buy. This task turned out to be an extraordinarily difficult one, for the many fleeing Christians passing through the city over the past several days had already taken the good animals with them. Finally he found one wretched, old, bony horse with one eye. Sensing his advantage, the crafty Moslem owner refused to bargain. He demanded an exorbitant price, and Frank had to pay it—several weeks' salary, in fact.

Preparations that evening had to be hasty and final. It was reminiscent of the Passover, as they ate their last supper in the little mud-walled house until— until, well, who could know when? Frank folded a quilt and put it under the saddle, just in case they should ever have a chance to rest. Behind the saddle he tied a bundle of clothes along with two small Persian carpets. Only recently Florence had been able to get a pair of brilliantly colored rugs. But now she looked at them not for their artistic value but for their practical potential. They might be traded for food in a crisis.

"Dear Floss, you've been so ill with the baby. I wish I could spare you this." Frank tightened the ropes around the bundles.

"Don't worry about me, Frank. We'll all go together, and God will give us strength. I've been asking Him all day for it," she said simply.

"But you'll get so tired holding the baby. Here, I think we can arrange something else." Frank found a board left over from the construction of his staircase. Swathed in blankets, the baby was placed on the board, securely tied between two pillows. Even her tiny face could be covered by a flap of her quilt. And already she slept!

Bundling on their own heaviest clothes, Frank and Florence were at last ready to go. Together they knelt. "Dear God, be with us this night as we go out. Protect and guide. Let us be hidden from the sight of the enemy. And be with our little home. We're just leaving it in Thy care." Frank prayed.

At the door they stopped and looked back. Their first home, with its homemade furniture. The lamp cast warm shadows and highlighted every loved, familiar object in the room. And so they went out into the midnight darkness.

Frank tied the precious baby bundle securely to the pommel of the saddle. They walked out to the north gate of the town. There they found the Russian army all ready to march. The commandant recognized Frank and directed him to fall into line where the wounded were being carried on stretchers between horses.

Silently the long line of refugees and the retreating army threaded its way up into the mountains that lay between Maragha and Tabriz. Frank trudged along beside the old horse, and everyone moved on alone with his own thoughts. Not a cigarette could be lighted, not a word spoken. Kurdish scouts might be anywhere there in the darkness to see and hear.

Suddenly, mounted guards rushed past them toward the rear—scouts had reported a stirring at the back of the group. The Kurds must have detected them and were perhaps overtaking them even now. Tense moments passed. Florence, already cold, felt she had frozen to the saddle. The column moved forward almost automatically, and no one seemed able to think.

But then, the tension passed. The guards slowly brought their rifles to rest, relaxed, and rode back to their places in the line. It had been a false alarm. Or so it seemed. But Florence could hardly restrain herself from crying for joy, "It's God doing it! He really isn't letting the Kurds see us." She wanted to shout.

The marchers moved on, the long human train driven steadily forward by the sheer instinct for self-preservation. Dawn came, the winter sun splashing itself across the mountain peaks and coursing down into the valleys. Noon was followed by afternoon, but not a moment could be taken for rest. No one could be sure how far north the Kurds might have penetrated. The mountains were their natural habitat. Here it would be hopeless for the marchers should the Kurds overtake them.

Darkness had just began to settle. Florence, nearly paralyzed with weariness, looked at Frank, who doggedly, endlessly paced beside her, his hand on the reins. She soon forgot herself and loved him all the more for what he meant to her.

Then without warning she felt a new movement in the old horse's plodding gait. Somehow there was a free, sliding motion under her. "Frank!" she gasped. And suddenly the saddle, quilt, rugs, baby bundle, and she herself all tumbled off the horse. The belly girt had loosened, and everything lay in a jumbled heap on the road.

Frank worked like a man possessed, trying to extricate Florence and the baby from the chaotic entanglement of their possessions. Everything had been so securely tied together, and now in the near-darkness their plight seemed hopeless. For the first time, Florence felt something akin to panic. The Russian army was moving on, leaving them behind. One after another the horses passed them. Soon they would be alone in the wilderness—prey to the Kurds!

"My God, help us!" she heard Frank mutter as he fought with the tangle of ropes. And at that moment a soldier noticed them and turned aside. With his bayonet he quickly cut the cords that held the cumbersome load. These he flung into the bushes by the road. No time to retie them now, and nothing could be left on the road to give the enemy a clue that the refugees had passed this way. Frank flung away the two rugs. Florence saw them go, but she registered no feeling at all. At such a time as this, nothing mattered except to get on the horse and start moving again.

Seeing that Frank had thrown many things away, the helpful soldier decided that the pillows were also unnecessary. So, with a wide sweep he threw the pillow bundle high over the bushes, out into the night.

Florence gasped as she saw the pillows arch high over the bank and drop out of sight into the ravine. A scream arose in her throat, and she clapped her hands over her mouth to choke it back. "Oh, my baby!" She almost strangled on the suppressed cry.

But already Frank had leaped over the rocks and disappeared down over the embankment. She could hear him down there in the dark. And then, miraculously, he was back by her side again with the pillows. Winona, still sandwiched onto the board, was unharmed. Mounting the horse again, Florence held the baby bundle in her arms, not willing to let it go even for an instant.

For three more days and nights the trek continued. Occasional rest stops were now possible, and the commandant showed the Osters great consideration. He always provided them with food and water, and by the time they neared Tabriz he arranged for Florence and the baby to ride in a two-wheeled cart he'd picked up in a village. Now Frank could ride the old horse.

"My feet hurt, Floss." It was the first admission Frank had made of any discomfort. "It's nice to ride." He grinned with great satisfaction.

Frank and Florence tried many times and in different ways to talk to the kind Russian commandant—in Turkish and in English, but to no avail. They learned that he could speak positively nothing but Russian.

"Floss, what do you think of that! Truly, he told me five days ago in Maragha that the Russian army would leave at midnight that night. And he said it in the clearest English," Frank marveled.

"Well, dear, I suppose it can mean only one thing," Floss ventured. "An angel must have spoken through him just at that moment to warn you and help us decide to leave Maragha."

"It must be that," Frank agreed. "We're living wholly in God's hands now—we have nothing else."

Upon reaching Tabriz, Frank and Florence found refuge with the Presbyterian missionaries at their compound. There too they found the American consul and other Americans gathered in a round-the-clock prayer service pleading for God's protection. The Kurds were expected in Tabriz momentarily.

And two days later they did come. But by this time the Russian army had received reinforcements and was ready for them. Swollen with their victories in the south, the Kurds confidently marched through Tabriz, not even stopping to plunder and kill. So, caught by surprise, they were quickly subdued by the Russians.

The Osters and other praying Christians watched the battle from the rooftops of the mission houses and saw the Kurds entirely put to flight. "It was just like watching the Lord win a battle for Israel, wasn't it?" Florence felt a new surge of wonder fill her.

So there they were—safe. God *had* heard. Some problems remained, of course. It took three months for Frank's bruised, blistered feet to heal. And all six of Florence's stitches that Dr. Joel had put in had come loose, and that job had to be done all over again.

The long-expected package of baby clothes from Chicago reached them during the brief respite between the departure of the Russians and the onslaught of the Kurds. With almost everything else lost in the flight to Tabriz, the parcel became a special boon for the refugees.

In Tabriz with fellow Christians they found a blessed retreat in very troubled times, and here Florence spent her second Persian Christmas.

The Lord Gives, and—

After a month of recuperating in Tabriz, Frank left Florence and the baby at the Presbyterian mission and returned to investigate the situation in Maragha. Although the danger of Kurdish reprisals seemed past, Frank still feared what he might discover there. The city had become almost a ghost town, a complete horror of destruction. Most of the houses in their neighborhood had been looted. "Many people were murdered here," a bystander informed him. What would he find in his own little house?

Frank stood at the entrance for a long moment before he entered, reluctant to see what he knew he might have to see. He opened the outer gate, crossed the garden, and waited again. Then, pushing the door open, he paused to allow his eyes to become adjusted to the darkness within. He realized with a start that everything was in its place—the house was exactly as they had left it! On the table stood a sooty lamp, and the walls, ceiling and curtains were black with soot. In their hasty flight they had forgotten and left the lamp burning.

Later when he described it to Florence, he said, "I just don't know *how* God managed it! Nor do I really know why I feared opening that door," he added sheepishly, "for, after all, we *had* left everything in His charge."

"Do you suppose," Florence speculated, "that He somehow used that smoking lamp to frighten the Kurds away from our house? I *wonder!*"

For the next four months Frank worked alone in Maragha, daily gleaning stories of providential deliverances of Christians all over the country during those terrible days of the killings. When he felt reasonably sure that the violence had indeed fully subsided, he returned to Tabriz.

"Floss! How good it is to be with you again, my little wife." He took her in his arms. "I've been very lonely."

"And baby and me too. Oh, Frank, the time's been very long. Have you come to take us home?" Florence's eyes swam with joyful tears.

"Yes, it's safe now. And, what's more," Frank smiled, "I have a surprise for you when you get there."

That surprise turned out to be a new house. Dr. Joel and his wife, after the frightful massacres of the Christmas season of 1914, had decided to move to a part of the country which was less chaotic for Christians. Frank had rented their Maragha house.

"Shall I carry you over the threshold like a bride?" Frank asked as the carriage stopped at the gate. Spring had come, and perhaps it was possible to be cheerful and have fun again.

"That won't be necessary," Florence laughed. "The neighbors might think it a little strange. But you can carry the baby in, if you like."

The house indeed turned out to be a great improvement over their first one—larger, cooler, and with plastered walls and ceilings. Moreover, the doors—or at least most of them—were high enough to walk through without bumping one's head. Floors were still of mud, but they were covered by carpets and clean sackcloth.

But problems pressed in on the Osters immediately! Maragha had filled with refugees, and over 600 of them were wholly destitute, having escaped with their lives and nothing more. The Osters had received a few hundred dollars of Red Cross funds from the Presbyterian missionaries in Tabriz, who had shared their windfall from America.

"How are we going to feed them when that money's gone," Florence wondered.

Frank shook his head. "I don't know. We've also used about fifty dollars of our own bread money already."

"But we just had to," Florence said. "Their need and suffering is so great. I don't think the outside world hears much about the troubles here, or more relief supplies would come through, I'm sure."

The city continued to be alive with rumors. The Russians had come down in great force and driven out the Turks, but instead of staying to consolidate their gains they had disappeared—no one knew where. So now news came that the Kurds were about to launch another invasion in the wake of this turn of events.

"Everything *seems* safe, Frank," Florence remarked. "But so many people advised against our returning to Maragha."

"Floss, our work is here," Frank said, as he looked at her steadily. "The Lord has shown us in so many ways in these past months that He's in charge of our affairs. We can only wait and trust. If there's trouble, we'll be shown what to do when the time comes."

Frank resumed his missionary trips to surrounding towns and villages. Winona thrived and brought Florence endless companionship and joy while Frank was away. Then summer came. Frank made Winona an indoor bed, complete with mattress, and also a roof bed that fitted over the foot of their cots under the mosquito net.

By her seventh month, the little girl was brightly aware of her surroundings. She knew the dog's name and squealed with delight when he played with her. At the word "Trixie" she would look out the window and start hunting for her playmate. Friends and neighbors, especially those who had shared the flight from the Kurds, loved the child dearly and insisted on taking turns holding her.

Then one day it all changed. Concern for the refugees, fear of the Kurds—it all paled into nothingness, as Frank and Florence concentrated on a terrifying personal crisis. Winona suddenly stopped nursing. She would take no water—nothing whatever. Her little fists clenched tightly, cutting right into the palms of her tiny hands, as she tossed her head back convulsively. Mother, father, dog—nothing interested her anymore.

Frantic, Frank and Florence watched over her day and night. With Dr. Joel gone, they had no medical assistance whatever. They pleaded with God to spare her life—their one treasure in a land that was barren of so many things.

"But, Floss," Frank always said gravely as they knelt in prayer, "we must always remember to ask for her life only if it is in God's will." Florence would nod her head in speechless anguish. "The Moslems have a word for it," Frank went on. "*Inshallah.*"

And then they would go on giving hot and cold treatments to relieve the spasms. Eleven days went by, and Winona grew steadily worse. "Floss, darling," Frank guided her toward the steps onto the roof. "You're so tired. Go up and rest, and let me watch for a while."

It seemed that Florence had barely kicked off her slippers and stretched herself out on the cot, head throbbing and eyes burning, when she heard Frank's voice at the door. A new note caught at her heart, and she rushed to the stairs. "Floss! Floss! Come quickly!"

Together they bent over the little homemade bed. "The end is near, Frank," she whispered. The fomentations and cool bathing this time did not stop the convulsions in the baby's thin little body. At last, the spasms did stop, and with them Winona's little heart also.

"The Lord gives and the Lord takes away." Yes, those were the words for occasions like this. Together they wept and prayed by the little bed and sought comfort and balm for their bleeding hearts in those words.

Where could they bury their little one? Not among the Moslems certainly—that was never permitted. And only orthodox members could be buried in the Armenian cemetery. They kept on praying. A neighbor helped Frank make a little coffin, and Florence sewed a tiny pillow from her wedding handkerchief. Here at last the sweet little head would rest.

Then the Armenian *keshish* came once again in answer to their need. He was the same friendly, generous priest who had welcomed them to Maragha almost two years before. He had heard of their sorrow and called at their home. Florence loved him for his kindly, fatherly ways, and he put his hand on her head and said, "My child, do not worry. She shall have a grave beside my own little girl."

And so the funeral was prepared. Together Frank and Florence wrapped Winona in one of the new blankets and placed her in the box, under the watchful, troubled gaze of Trixie, with whom she would romp no more. With a last loving look, they closed the lid. Frank, along with many men, proceeded to the cemetery; but since Persian women never go to funerals, Florence remained at home with the women.

As they sat together, instead of listening to the weeping and wailing of hired mourners, the guests heard Florence quietly explain her hope of the resurrection. And at the graveside on that late August afternoon, Frank and the *keshish* conducted the short service.

The exchange of letters with the family at home was slow, and when messages of sympathy eventually came from loving aunts and grandparents, the wound opened afresh. This went on for several weeks. Even faith, hope, and the pressure of their work could not spare them the loneliness. Both of them dreamed of the child almost every night, for she had taken deep root in their hearts. Florence folded up the baby things—every piece almost like a living part of herself—and put them away. But at the same time her heart reached up to God in a very simple prayer, "Give us another baby, Lord, if it be Thy will."

Now a full schedule of missionary work occupied their days; Frank and Florence refused to let their loneliness and sorrow overwhelm them. Four days weekly, Florence went over to teach English and sewing at the Armenian school—an appointment which ultimately enabled her to win some children to the Adventist faith.

Frank went on holding meetings twice each Sunday in their home, and on other evenings he gave Bible studies in various homes. They would look at the almost 100 persons crowded into their parlor, occupying even the windowsills and doorways, and wonder why results were so long in coming. Then they would remind one another of God's time clock and try to be patient.

Meanwhile, the Oster home was at once a free hotel and a hospital. One man lay sick on their couch for two weeks, his fever climbing to 105°. During his three-day delirium, Frank watched over him day and night, sponging him with cool water. He finally got well, but before he left a family arrived from Sāūjbulāgh (Mahābād). The man was blind; his wife and the four-month-old twins were ill. One of them had a hideous, oozing ulcer covering most of her face, and her runny eyes were swollen shut. The Osters put them all to bed and nursed and treated each one. Florence had almost twenty-four-hour duty in trying to meet the demanding needs of the twins. One of the twins finally died, but the rest of the family recovered and at last were able to go to a home of their own.

"Frank, we desperately need some medical help here. How are

we going to be able to do everything?" Florence sometimes felt staggered by it all.

"I know, Floss, but it will come some day. I'm sure of it," Frank said with conviction. It was just as well, perhaps, that they couldn't know that they would wait another ten years before this prediction would come true.

Those days halfway through the war were often dark, but then something happened to brighten the horizon in the Oster home. For three or four months Florence had continued to pray her special little prayer, "God, give us another child, please, if it's Thy will." Tired and discouraged as she sometimes was, she clung to this hope. And then one day they knew they could plan for another little one to arrive in the middle of the next summer.

Florence didn't feel exactly well during this time, and often wished she could see a good doctor. Her happy anticipation, however, prevented her from dreading the ordeal. "After all, God is our physician, so surely we don't have to worry."

As the time for the baby's arrival neared, Frank decided Florence should be in a hospital. "Floss," he said one day, "I think we should take you up to the Presbyterian mission hospital in Tabriz where you can have proper attention."

Florence agreed, relieved in fact, that he had suggested it. Having to depend on a Persian midwife would be an appalling experience for her, she knew.

According to Persian custom, during delivery the mother was required to sit on a pile of *yapmah* (manure cakes) over a pan of ashes. Following delivery she lay in the ashes for twenty-four hours, and for seven days following the mother was allowed not a drop of water. It made no difference how hot the weather or how feverish she became. The babies themselves never got a drop of water until they were a year old. Their beginning in the world seemed unpromising, to be sure. Upon arrival they received a sip of the mother's urine, for tonic purposes, and then they were placed in a napkin filled with warm sand. This was changed twice daily, but they weren't bathed. Infant mortality ran high, and Florence knew one mother who had only one living child out of twenty-one pregnancies!

No matter how great the crisis, no Persian woman would call a man doctor for a delivery, even if she were dying. One desperate husband had approached one of the Tabriz mission doctors pleading for some medicine for his wife, who had been in labor for days. Naturally, the doctor could not administer medicine without seeing his patient. Rather than permit the doctor to see his wife, however, the man went sorrowfully away to watch the death of the mother and the unborn baby.

Frank hired a closed carriage—a great luxury—and they arrived in Tabriz in just two days. They couldn't forget, of course, their last trip in mid-winter with the bony old horse and the retreating Russian army. This journey, however, was a festive one.

In Tabriz they rented a room, did their own cooking, and relaxed for three weeks. Dr. Vaneman gave skillful service, and little Winton Byington Oster arrived just after noon on July 13, 1916. He didn't even interrupt a night's sleep for his parents.

As usual, this happy domestic event was almost immediately offset by public problems again. War conditions had worsened noticeably, and people again fled from Maragha. Moreover, a cholera epidemic raged all through the area east of Lake Urmia.

Never one to be idle. Frank soon had a number of Bible studies under way in Tabriz, sometimes as many as three or four a day. Florence wondered how long they would be confined to that little rented room.

One day a letter from home arrived full of news about camp meeting. "Would't it be nice to go to camp meeting again, Frank?" Florence indulged herself in a little dreaming while she hemmed a nightgown for the baby.

"Perhaps we can again some day, Floss. I think about it too sometimes," Frank admitted. He had been away from home for seven years.

"Of course, we came out here for life," Florence quickly put in. "I truly love our work, and I've never regretted coming. Please understand." She did not want Frank to think even for a moment that her resolution had weakened, but home—it tugged at her feelings often.

"Well, someday, Floss. Perhaps when the war's over we can have a visit back to America."

The immediate future continued uncertain until one day the American consul in Tabriz advised Frank to forget Maragha and move his family permanently to Tabriz. "There's constant unrest down there. With the continuing threat of the Kurds, it just isn't safe."

Wisdom being indeed the better part of valor, Frank left in early October to pack up their household goods in Maragha and bring them back to Tabriz.

But while he was solving one problem, another, still more serious, arose.

Trials and Triumphs

Florence awoke one morning feeling decidedly indisposed. She got up to attend to the crying baby, but she felt dizzy and light-headed. Taking him with her, she got back into bed to rest a little longer. Perhaps later, she thought, the miserable feeling would pass. By noon, however, her fever had shot up, and by late afternoon it soared still higher. She felt worse than she could remember ever having felt in her whole life.

Finally she had to give in and send for Dr. Vaneman. His diagnosis wasn't new. Typhoid had struck again. A missionary neighbor came to help Florence and baby Winton.

When Frank returned from Maragha, he found a hospital established in his own small room—the mother sick and the baby seemingly ill too at times. Hastily he located a house to rent, moved in the household goods, and moved his two patients there. Waiting on them both, he resumed his sickroom duties.

"Frank, I think I shouldn't nurse the baby anymore. I must be infecting him," Florence said one morning. "And I'm tired—so tired." Her voice trailed off, and she lay back hardly knowing or caring. Thoughts of the baby drifted fuzzily through her mind. And poor Frank! How much work he had again, but—and she lapsed off into another stupor.

"Don't worry, Floss, I'll figure out something," Frank promised.

First he hired a *dayah* (wet nurse) who, for a price, would nurse Winton along with her own baby. When Frank discovered her smoking one day, however, he promptly dismissed her. "I'll not have tobacco poisons circulating through the body of *my* young son," he told her.

Dr. Vaneman wrote out a milk formula for Winton, and Frank invented a fairly commendable feeding bottle by attaching a nipple to a beer bottle. But now, how about the milk itself?

The woman who sold them fresh milk had a habit of diluting it with water. But what water! He knew very well the source of her supply. It was an open ditch where women scrubbed clothes, children played, farmers washed down their animals, and dogs got drinks. In fact, Osters had the same water stored in the *ab-ambar* (cistern) under the house. Of course, they'd always boiled it—vigorously, and for a long time.

Dealing with the impure milk now presented Frank with other problems. The matter had to be handled with tact, but also he had to be *sure* that mistakes weren't made. Calling the helper boy, he said, "Anonia, take these two buckets to the milk lady, please. Tell her that we prefer mixing our own milk. One pail is for the milk, and the other is for the water."

When the lad explained Frank's orders to the astonished woman, she cried incredulously, "What does he want to do that for?" The fact that he could see through her shrewd little practice mortified her.

"I don't know. He said he wants to mix them himself."

"*Ay havar!* These foreigners! *Ajeeb* [strange]," she grumbled. "They're so queer."

Anonia agreed—they were full of the most peculiar notions. "But that's what he wants anyway," he insisted. So the woman filled one pail with milk and the other with water, muttering all the while about the perversity of foreigners.

When the boy re-appeared at the kitchen door, Frank took both buckets. "Thank you, Anonia. This will do very well." Then, after throwing out the water, he pasteurized the milk, made up the formula, and filled Winton's beer bottle. So the new feeding station went into business.

After twenty-one feverish days, Florence began to feel better. She even had a little appetite. But somehow what she ate sent her into a serious relapse. In three more weeks she seemed to be recovering again, when she went down with a still more critical relapse. For a total of two months she didn't recognize Winton, give him a thought, or know that he existed.

Day and night, Frank shuttled between Florence's bedside and the baby crib, and making formula in the kitchen. Dr. Vaneman called one day to see the patient. Taking one look at Florence, he turned to Frank and said gently, "Florence is in such a critical condition now, Frank, that you shouldn't expect too much. Actually, I really didn't think she'd pull through that first relapse. And this is much worse."

"But with God all things are possible." Frank reached out for hope.

"True. Very true," the good doctor replied. "And now we've reached that point. It's all in His hands."

Frank sat by the bed looking at Florence, a mere shadow now of the happy girl he'd promised to cherish "in sickness and in health" back there in London. Was that only four years ago? But God had led in so many remarkable ways in those years, and they had dedicated their entire lives to His service in Persia. And now the doctor said it could be the end—already.

Frank had prayed for weeks, but somehow now—just now—might God truly heal her? His mind went back to those times when he and Florence had pleaded with the Lord for the life of Winona. He had always added that important qualifying phrase, "If it be Thy will." And the answer had come back, No. Frank knew that in the prayer he would offer now, he would have to say those same words. Struggling with his exhausted emotions, he dropped to his knees by the bed and took Florence's hand.

"Dear God, heal my Floss. Do it just now, so that she can continue to work with me here in Persia. Give us not according to our deserving but according to the multitude of Thy tender mercies. Lord, it's not my will. Let *Thy* will be done."

Frank waited, then finally opened his eyes and got up. Florence was watching him. "Frank," she whispered, "I felt so very strange just now."

He bent over her. "I was praying for you, Floss."

"Yes, I know. I had a kind of whirling feeling." She smiled, a very small smile, but Frank saw it and his heart leaped for joy. When he laid his hand on her forehead, he found it cool.

Recovery came slowly but steadily. After three months Dr. Vaneman declared her cured. She remained weak, of course; and for the first four weeks she couldn't walk, but crawled around the room on her hands and knees.

Then her hair began falling out—long strands of the chestnut waves lay on her pillow every day. "Oh, Frank," she wailed, as she looked at her pale, haggard form and her rapidly balding head in the mirror. "I look terrible. Just dreadful!"

Frank laughed and picked up her too-light frame and swung her down into a chair. "Don't say silly things, Floss. To me you're beautiful."

"Frank, you're sweet, but the mirror doesn't lie," Florence countered sadly.

"Still," he declared, "you're alive, I'm alive, we're in love, we have a fine healthy son, and the world's before us—and I say that's all beautiful!"

The hair situation finally reached the point where Florence cut off the last scanty tuft that remained and donned a hat until nature could make the necessary repairs.

On March 11, 1917, after Florence's seven months of confinement, Frank said one afternoon, "Let's take a carriage ride to celebrate your birthday. You're twenty-nine today, you know. And you do seem much stronger now." So they rode out through the city streets and into the countryside, which seemed almost ready to erupt into spring. Florence delighted in every detail—the least color, the faintest bird song. Everything thrilled her, for she felt as one who had returned from the dead.

The carriage returned to their door, and Florence alighted. Turning to her escort, she said, "Thank you, Frank. It was a lovely ride."

"You're so very welcome, my dear!" Frank gallantly opened the door and ushered her into the house. "I'm happy to do anything at all to please a sweet miracle-wife like you."

Florence hesitated. "But, Frank, it's so dark in here. What—"

"I guess we'll have to light a lamp then," Frank said, as he urged her on in.

Just then a chorus of voices filled the room. "Happy birthday, Florence." All of their Presbyterian missionary friends had come to celebrate her birthday with her. Florence sank into a chair and wept—life seemed almost *too* good. It was fun—yes, blessed fun—just to be alive and have friends and be loved. No one at all noticed that she kept her hat on all through the party.

Once again, things in the Oster home settled into tranquillity.

Frank's meetings were well attended, and a few people had begun to keep the Sabbath. At nine months Winton still thrived on Frank's beer-bottle formula. He could scoot across the carpets faster than Florence could chase him. He turned up the corners of the rugs, and with the help of his two new teeth, tasted the dirt floor every chance he got.

Then a smallpox epidemic broke out in Tabriz. The mild winter had brought little rain but much sickness. Dr. Vaneman saved the last of his vaccine for the Osters.

The war still raged, and during the third year, restrictions and privations began to increase noticeably. The price of sugar reached a dollar seventy-five a pound, and later it became five dollars a pound. Before the war ended, sugar disappeared from the market altogether. Florence made a dessert about once a year. Of course, they still had to hoard a little sugar for when company came and the hospitality cup of tea had to be served from the *samovar* (charcoal-heated teapot). Failure to serve tea to guests, the Osters had learned by trial and error, was a gross breach of Persian etiquette. From Russian friends Florence learned to make delicious fig tea; so they could demonstrate their health principles in regard to tea-drinking. Many of their acquaintances, and even the governor of Tabriz, learned to make and enjoy fig tea. With cooking oil going at fifty cents a liter, Florence resorted to sheep fat. She bought the long tails of the fat-tailed sheep at the market, put them in a pot over the fire, and when the fat melted from the tails it was used for cooking. Fresh fruit became scarce and high priced, and she had to confine the menus to native foods.

Clothes, too, posed a problem. Florence had had no new clothes since she married, but finally she had to give in and buy material for a new coat. At five dollars a yard, the cloth was the cheapest she could find. Everything seemed to be wearing out, and Florence worried about how they would meet the needs of the next winter. Before that time came, Frank simply *had* to spend twenty dollars for a new pair of shoes—after all, he couldn't go barefoot.

The European Division transferred money in periodically, but Frank and Florence used it most sparingly. They had received no financial statement for two years, and as far as they knew they were still in the same wage bracket Elder Conradi had determined for them—nine dollars fifty cents per week.

By now two Persians had become Seventh-day Adventists, and Florence and Frank discovered three Sabbath keepers among the Russian soldiers. One of the men spoke German. The Osters could converse freely with him; but the others could speak and understand only Russian. However, these linguistic limitations proved to be little hindrance to good times and good fellowship together.

By mid-summer, inflation had driven prices completely out of sight. Potatoes sold for eleven dollars a sack. What the Kurds had not done, starvation might yet accomplish. A severe summer drought brought everyone face to face with famine. People waited for hours at the bakery to buy bread—and had to pay bribes for whatever they got. Much of the time they waited for nothing. The bread sold out before they reached the head of the line. Violence broke out; and bakers as well as customers, from time to time, were beaten to death.

Florence made her last two sacks of flour into a month's supply of *lavash!* "I hope that when this is gone," she told Frank, "we can find more wheat somewhere to grind into flour."

Almost daily Frank brought home bad news. Whole bazaars in Urmia and Kazvin (Qazvin) had been destroyed and plundered. "People have real fears here that Tabriz will be next," he said. The pressures of the war were pushing the whole country into famine and violence.

Yet it never occurred to either Frank or Florence to consider trying to go to the States. In fact, a letter did come from headquarters offering them furlough. "Floss, how can we go?" Although most of the other missionaries had evacuated by now, as citizens of neutral Switzerland, they could stay on. Frank flew the Swiss flag at their gate as a matter of policy.

Florence thought of the tiny church company. The war multiplied their problems. However, after all these years, the church in Persia seemed just on the threshold of its life. "No, Frank. You're right. God's work will suffer if we leave. We can't go now—I can see that."

"Perhaps we can soon get a replacement. Meanwhile, we'll stay by our post of duty." Florence admired Frank for his devotion—a loyalty unmatched perhaps on any of the war fronts.

Then an experience at the Presbyterian mission compound in

Urmia underscored the need to be constant in service, especially in these days of war. It made the Osters realize that they hadn't yet begun to probe the depths and magnitude of the challenge of Persia.

A Christian had one day encountered a Kurd in the foothills. When they had exchanged greetings, the Kurd astonished the man by asking, "What do you Christians believe?"

Surprised and fearful, the Christian stared at him. Was this a trap of some kind? Then, very simply, he told of Jesus, His great sacrifice, and His promise of forgiveness and salvation.

The mountain outlaw fell silent for a time, deep in thought. "How do you become a Christian?"

"If you believe, you must be baptized. Then you're a Christian," the man said.

Determined to know more, the next day the Kurd mounted his pony and rode down to Urmia where there were several Christian missions. Most of the things he had heard were confused in his mind, but one idea stuck: "You must be baptized, and then you're a Christian."

He knocked at the gate of the Presbyterian mission and Dr. Allen opened the door. Naturally, the sight of a Kurd in his tribal dress made the missionary recoil in terror.

"I want to be a Christian. Will you baptize me?"

Dr. Allen hesitated. A horde of Kurds might well be around the corner, with this man as a decoy, waiting to gain an entrance to the compound.

"You may come in and go into our chapel," Dr. Allen invited, hesitantly. They walked toward the small church. "Of course, you'll need to join a baptismal class and study the Bible. And then, if you're faithful, you may be baptized." He opened the door and ushered the Kurd in. "And now, if you'll wait here a moment, I'll be back shortly."

The doctor hurried off to investigate who the man might be and why he had come. That took some time.

Meanwhile, the would-be-Christian Kurd grew impatient and left the compound. Accosting a boy on the street, he said, "Are there any other Christian missions here?"

"Over there." The lad pointed to another complex of flat-roofed mud buildings. "That's the Catholic mission."

A priest answered his knock this time. "Will you baptize me?" The Kurd repeated his question. "I want to be a Christian."

Taking him by the hand and drawing him quickly inside, the priest bolted the door. "Yes, my brother. Let's talk about it now."

Shortly after, he baptized the Kurd. Then, knowing that he'd be killed if he should go again into his home in the mountains of Kurdistan, the convert remained at the mission.

A few weeks later the Kurds poured down out of the mountains on another raid to kill Christians and plunder their property in Urmia. Arriving at the Catholic mission, they were amazed to find one of their own number there. "Why are you here? The Christian dogs! Have they captured you? Fear not," they promised him cheerfully, "we're here to free you and punish your persecutors."

"No, my brothers," the Kurd replied, "I am now a Christian, and I belong here."

"A Christian!" they cried in utter disbelief. "Now surely, you don't mean that. Come with us. You've been bewitched."

They beat him unmercifully in an attempt to persuade him of his error, but all he would say was, "I love my Saviour. I cannot deny Him."

"We're out on a *jihad* [holy war]," the leader announced darkly. "The sword of Islam has again been unsheathed and all must submit or be killed."

The Christian Kurd knew only too well that this was how Moslem converts were often made, but he persisted in his stand for his new-found Lord. "Then we must do with you as we do with all the other Christians." So saying, they bound him and took him out into the street.

On the way to the main gate of the city, they picked up four other Christian men. Then they hanged all five of them in the gate—the Kurd in the middle facing outward, so that every Kurd who passed by would be reminded of the reward awaiting those who changed their religion. The other Christians flanked him on either side, facing toward the city as a warning to those who might attempt to leave town.

Next, the party of Kurds stopped at the American orphanage operated by Mr. and Mrs. Pflaumer. Along with Miss Bridges, a fellow missionary, they daily cared for more than forty Moslem and Christian orphans.

Having battered down the walls, the Kurds poured into the compound, destroying what they couldn't carry and killing many of the children. The three missionaries tried to hide, but without success. One of the most fearsome-looking Kurds caught sight of Miss Bridges. Seizing her by the arm, he shouted, "Come with me!"

Knowing what this order would lead to, Mr. Pflaumer leaped forward and flung his arms around the girl and pulled her back.

"Let her go, I tell you!" screamed the Kurd, striking him a blow on the back with his rifle butt.

The missionary stood his ground. "We cannot keep you from carrying away Armenian girls or murdering them, but we're Americans. You cannot—you *will* not—do this thing!"

The crazed Kurd's fury lashed into a tempest. "Armenian or American, it makes no difference to me! I will have the woman for my harem, do you see?" And with that, he leveled his gun and shot Mr. Pflaumer at point-blank range. The missionary collapsed at the girl's feet.

Putting her on his horse and throwing a blanket over her blood-stained dress, the Kurd led the girl off without even a backward glance at the stricken Mrs. Pflaumer, who had fallen on her knees, her arms around her husband's lifeless body in the courtyard. Was this what it would take to get a Christian missionary into Kurdistan? Miss Bridges shuddered and looked down with horror at the vicious man leading the horse.

They had not gone far, when she recognized a Turkish officer. True, he was one who had accompanied the Kurds on the raid, a leader and instigator, no doubt. Still, she cried out to him, *"Mani gurtar!* [Save me!]."

The Turk looked at her closely and halted the Kurd. "What is this you have?"

"A woman—nothing but a woman," the Kurd muttered sullenly.

"But she's an American woman," the Turk replied. "We can't do this to Americans—we might get into real trouble." He reached up to help her off the horse. "Go find another woman, but don't make this mistake again," he advised the Kurd.

The Turkish officer conducted her safely back to the orphanage, where they found Mrs. Pflaumer still alone, prostrate, over her murdered husband. Both women went to the governor's mansion for safety, and as soon as travel became possible, they went to

Tabriz. Once again, the Osters took in refugees, this time their own countrymen—Mrs. Pflaumer and Miss Bridges.

When the Kurds had finally plundered until virtually nothing of value remained, and when they had satiated their appetite for killing, they departed. Then the missionaries had the task of coming out to clear away the debris and to bury the dead.

Along with some of his helpers, Dr. Allen began carrying several slain Christians out of the city for burial. They saw the five bodies hanging in the gate. As they passed under the dangling feet, the missionary looked up into the face of the central figure, clad in Kurdish dress. He recognized him as the man who had pleaded with him for baptism!

Quickly laying down his burden, the doctor climbed up and cut the rope by which the dead man hung. Reverently he laid him on the ground and bent over him, weeping.

In telling the story to the Osters later, great tears filled the doctor's eyes again. "Frank, when I looked into that man's face," he said, "I had to kneel down by him and beg his forgiveness." In the choked silence, none of them could speak; and then the missionary went on. "And I said to him, 'Brother Kurd, I thought you weren't ready to live for Christ, but I see that you were ready to die for Him.' May God forgive my doubting!"

The massacres went on. Hardships and difficulties multiplied as the world moved into the last agonizing year of the war. But never, no matter what the circumstances, did Frank and Florence forget the lesson taught them by the Kurd who died a Christian. Who could ever dare put an estimate on the value of a human soul—even that of a Kurd! Progress in seven years seemed *so* small to Frank and Florence. Yet, after this long time of planting, surely God would reap a harvest among these people.

The End of an Era

The trauma of the war reached its peak in May 1918. With Russia still occupying Azerbaijan and the English build-up of strong influence in the south, the situation in Persia became highly incendiary. Assisted by their old allies the Kurds, the Turks invaded Persia. The Assyrian Christians in Urmia, supported by arms and ammunition from the French army, put up a valiant fight, but to no avail. When French support had to be withdrawn, the 80,000 inhabitants of Urmia decided to evacuate.

Dr. W. A. Shedd, supervisor of the Presbyterian mission, became acting American consul for the area, and under his leadership the vast host of Christians fled south. The men, heavily armed, surrounded the group of women and children and fought off the enemy on every side. But then cholera broke out, and the dead and dying had to be left beside the road as the wretched lines of marchers pressed on. Dr. Shedd himself collapsed by the roadside, and a few hours later his wife and two helpers opened a shallow grave with their bare hands and buried the missionary doctor.

In Tabriz the Osters became involved with a number of refugees as the tragedies of war multiplied. Ten-year-old Esnet arrived at the little Adventist school in Tabriz having already lived through more than a lifetime of terror. On the long march she had walked with her younger brother and her mother, who carried the baby on her back. Father marched with the defenders on the outskirts of the company. First Esnet noticed that the baby had been shot. Mother untied him and left him beside the road. A few hours later a stray bullet killed her little brother. Two days later, as she and her mother walked hand in hand, she felt a sudden tremor go through her mother's body. Looking up, she realized that her mother too had been shot. When she eventually reached Tabriz, she found her father again, but not for long. Severely wounded, he died soon afterward. Frank performed the funeral service and brought the lone little Esnet back home with him.

Teenager Julia Oraham had remained behind in Urmia with her father, a medical doctor. His services were needed for the older people, who had not been able to evacuate. As the enemy approached, the Christians retreated to their churches to pray for deliverance. Julia joined the more than 250 people in the Presbyterian church. But when the Turks found them, they hewed them down with their swords, not wanting to waste bullets. In the slaughter Julia rushed through the door, rolled down the steps over a heap of dead bodies and escaped into a Moslem home. Her father was shot in his home, as he lay ill in bed. Finally Julia reached the American orphanage in Tabriz.

Frank and Florence dealt with each desperate case as it came along. These two girls, Esnet and Julia, along with others like them, eventually made their way into the Seventh-day Adventist Church. The terrors of war brought unique opportunities for ministry. Although the Osters could not realize it at the time, they were actually training, in this tragically difficult school of suffering the future workers for the church in Persia.

Relentlessly the Turks and Kurds scourged the country from Urmia to Tabriz. In their efforts to drive the Russians out of Azerbaijan, the Turkish army steadily bore down on Tabriz—to the intense apprehension of the Christian population there.

During one of his hospital visits to see wounded Russian soldiers—of which Tabriz now had large numbers—Frank found a soldier suffering not with wounds but with pneumonia. The man could speak neither English nor Turkish, but the soldier opened his Bible to Exodus 20 and pointed to the fourth commandment. Frank got the message; the man was a Seventh-day Adventist! They learned his name was Knish.

"Floss, the Russians are about to evacuate the city," Frank said one day. "I think we should bring Brother Knish home with us. He'll certainly be left behind."

Florence had nursed so many patients on her living-room couch, on the floor, on the roof—nothing could surprise her now. "By all means, Frank. We must make a place for him here."

It was not likely that the Russian army would ever entertain a very high opinion of Knish's value as a soldier. In training camp before he came to Tabriz, he had refused the commanding officer's order to take up his gun. "Did you not hear the command to take up the weapon?" the lieutenant roared.

"Yes, sir," Knish replied, "but I cannot kill, therefore, I cannot take up the gun."

"Pick up that weapon! This is your last chance." The officer turned white with fury. "Russia is at war. Foolish whims will not be tolerated."

Knish remained firm. The commander's czarist training had taught him no other solution for dealing with an insubordinate soldier, so he raised his sword high. When he brought it down for the death blow, however, it doubled over, shattered into fragments, and fell to the ground.

Speechless with fury, he ordered the sergeant to take Knish to the guardhouse. Here, in the cold and damp, the prisoner spent long hours tied to a fence post outside in the cold. He contracted pneumonia. Had it not been for the kindness and care of Frank and Florence he no doubt never would have pulled through.

With the Turks now riding into Tabriz, Frank was at his wit's end to know how to protect the sick Russian in his house. If he were found, they'd all be killed—no question about that. Nothing but prayer—and the brave Swiss flag at the gate! The Turks actually did enter the compound, but for some divinely appointed reason, they neglected to search either the mission buildings or the Oster home.

Communication with Brother Knish was severely limited, but he learned some Turkish, and Frank and Florence added a little more to their meager Russian. And with a few English words to fill in here and there, they managed to enjoy a surprising degree of fellowship. The Osters made the delightful discovery that their captive guest was an artist.

On November 11, 1918, with the signing of the Armistice, five months of Turkish occupation ended. Brother Knish had his freedom again, and the battle-scarred population of northwestern Persia began to consider what life might be like without war.

During this long confinement Knish painted a large portrait of the Shah of Persia. He presented it to the king in person, and it so pleased the ruler on the ancient Peacock Throne of Persia that he gave him a large gift of money—enough to enable him to travel back to his home in Russia.

War's end, however, didn't bring instantaneous relief from the famine which the war and two years without rain had brought. Still, on Thanksgiving Day, Florence wanted to declare her thankfulness in some tangible way. After all, the war *was* over, and they also had another son. Francis Frederick had joined them on July 15, 1918. Not only had God preserved their lives through the terrible years, He had also increased their number.

So she invited two dozen boys and girls to eat their fill of soup, potatoes and bread. She knew for a certainty that the children had not eaten a decent meal in months. Two-and-a-half-year-old Winton, not to be outdone by his mother's hospitality, conducted his own charity on the sly. Awareness of the scarcity of food in his own house made him hesitate to dispense food openly. One day Florence pointed out some children gathering leaves.

"Look, Winton," his mother said. "Those poor little boys out there have nothing to eat. They're picking up leaves by the compound wall to make soup.

A few minutes later Florence happened to glance out the window. She saw Winton sidling out through the yard, trying to hide two sheets of *lavash* behind his wholly inadequate small back. She watched him give them to the boys with that big smile which is reserved for the use of Good Samaritans everywhere.

Another kind of famine also raged. Frank and Florence felt that they were slowly starving for the want of mail. For twelve months the international blockade had separated them from their family in America and South Africa. In a year the old letters had been read and re-read, and then Florence would start all over again. They had become so yellowed and dog-eared that they almost looked like museum documents—and for Florence they practically were.

Then on December 4, 1918, Frank came home with a huge bag on his back. "Floss, come and look." His voice had a sharp new note of exultation she hadn't heard for a long time, and it brought her running. He upended the gunny sack and an avalanche of mail tumbled out over the living room floor.

"Frank! Frank! Do you mean it!" She threw herself on the floor, into the midst of the heap. No longer was she the mother of two sons, the wife of a pastor, the nurse of refugees, the teacher of orphans. She was only a very small girl now, weeping for joy. "Here's a letter from Mother! And another! And three more!" She gasped between sobs and squeals of joy. "And four from Vandella already." She pushed the magazines and packages aside, and built up the colorful stack of personal letters, pawing through them like a beaver building a dam.

Frank smiled down at her where she sat on the floor. He'd never seen her quite like this before. She had been through so much in five years. "Let's start with the latest letters and read backwards, Floss," he suggested.

Florence had already grouped the letters by postmarks. "Oh, no! We might miss something. We must start with the earliest and read forward."

Frank laughed and sat down beside her, while Winton romped through the packages. One way or another they read the mail—forward, backward, and in the middle. It made no difference.

Although the "great mail flood" kept the Osters in a kind of emotional paradise for days, grim realities still surrounded them. With funds provided by the Near East Relief Foundation, Frank carried on an extensive welfare work.

Typhus followed hard on the heels of the famine in a fatal kind of chain reaction. Even with dogs and cats and some of the rats gone, lice and the rest of the rats could still carry the disease. Masses of refugees crowded into concentration camps and mission compounds, and sanitation fell to an all-time low. Every time Frank got into a phaeton he was helpless to ward off the army of lice that crawled up his trouser legs and shirt sleeves.

Already three returned Presbyterian missionaries had died of typhus. "We *must* be careful, Frank." Florence fought daily battles on the home front to keep the house germ free.

When Frank arrived home, he would undress in a shed outside, shake his clothes out over a fire, fumigate his entire body and clothes, and take a shower. Florence always had clean clothes waiting for him in the shed. But even these precautions proved to be insufficient.

One day Frank came home with a fever. Was he to become another statistic in the epidemic? For two weeks the disease raged, and he tossed in delirium most of the time. In his tortured mind he still worked, preaching at an endless series of evangelistic meetings.

"Floss," he would call. "Please dismiss the people so I can rest. I'm so tired."

Florence would stand and say, "Let's pray." Then, having pronounced the benediction, she would dismiss the people and invite them to return the next day. Opening the bedroom door she would bid the imaginary congregation farewell and usher them out. Frank could relax at last.

But a few minutes later she would hear him launching into another Turkish sermon, talking until he was exhausted. "Ah, Floss," he groaned. "I'm so tired. Send them home please." And she would go through the procedure again. He could never rest until the congregation had been formally ushered out of the room. But no sooner had she started to tend to the baby or look after other household chores than she would hear him again. *"Chokh khosh galdiz, aziz doostlarmiz* . . . [Welcome again, my friends]." And he was off into another sermon.

Dr. Vaneman made two to four house calls a day. When Frank wasn't preaching, he lay in a half-stupor. At three o'clock one morning his feet suddenly became cold and stiff. Frightened, Florence brought hot water bottles and used friction to get the circulation going again.

Now she realized that if she carried on the battle for his life alone, she might well lose. Kind friends took the little boys in charge, and a missionary nurse spent the nights with her. The nurse took over the vigil about 1 a.m. so that Florence could get a little rest.

One evening when Dr. Vaneman called, he studied his patient carefully and said, "Florence, you let me sit up with Frank tonight, and you go into the other room and have a good sleep."

Exhausted, and confident that Frank was in good hands, Florence dropped off to sleep and knew nothing until sunrise. She rushed to the bedroom. "How is he, doctor?"

Dr. Vaneman looked grave. "Well, Florence, you didn't realize it, but the reason I stayed was that I didn't expect him to last through the night. I didn't want you to be here all alone."

Once again the words were spoken in the Oster house. "We cannot expect much—he's in God's hands." Soon after the doctor left, Florence heard wailing in the courtyard outside—the sounds of the death-wail which she had come to know so well. Apparently the doctor had not given inquirers in the compound an optimistic report when he went out. Medical science could do no more, and immunization against typhus was still many years down the road.

Florence stood looking at her husband—inert and unaware. Would he ever get up again? She wondered. Under the window the wailing crescendoed, and she went to the front door. "Don't weep, my friends. He's not dead." Her voice choked. "But please pray with me that he may yet recover."

Back inside she knelt by Frank's bed and laid her hand over his, in a complete reversal of the scene where Frank had knelt by her bed two-and-a-half years before. The same bed, the same need, and the same prayer. "Lord, heal him. Allow him to continue Thy work in Persia," she said. Then she added those words which she and Frank had long ago agreed must be part of every prayer request, "if it be Thy will."

As she rose from her knees, Frank opened his eyes and looked at her. There was but the faintest trace of recognition, but it held out promise to Florence. Slow as it was, recovery came at last.

Florence told Frank about all the Turkish sermons he had preached during the early part of his illness. "You know, Floss, it's an odd thing. I learned to preach in Armenian first—I wonder why it came out in Turkish now?"

"I don't know, Frank," Florence replied, "but they were powerful sermons. But you never could get through to the end of them, poor boy." Florence sat on the foot of the bed watching him drink his soup.

"I've been thinking about it, Floss," Frank said, looking puzzled. "I don't seem to know any Armenian words anymore. It's as if the whole vocabulary has gone right out of my head." And so it had, for Frank never was able to use the Armenian language again for the rest of his life.

Frank finished his very small supper, but it made Florence happy to see him eat anything at all. She took his tray, but remained seated on the bed. "Do you know what Dr. Vaneman's going to tell you one of these days?" she asked.

"Well, no, not exactly!" Frank looked up, surprised. "But I suppose I could think of one or two things, maybe."

"He's going to tell you to take a rest—a furlough. To go home, Frank."

"And he would be right, Floss." She could see that he struggled with a heavy thought. "We both need it, I think. Still, we've got the same problem. How can we leave our work here? If only there were just one more Seventh-day Adventist family here in Persia."

"I know. Someone should be here to hold the post while we're gone." But Florence considered a new version of the prayer they'd prayed so often. "Perhaps this is a decision that we should not take too much upon ourselves alone. God knows the need, and I think we ought to pray and ask Him whether or not it's time for us to take a furlough—let *Him* indicate His will in the matter."

That night Florence wrote to the European Division, explaining their present situation and urgently requesting that another worker be sent. Together they studied the letter. "It's all right, Floss," Frank agreed. "They will decide now what we should do."

"And of course," Florence added, "our going will be only temporary. Persia is now home more than anywhere else. Our hearts are always here no matter where else we might ever be."

Frank lay back on the pillows, contented. "We'd only be accepting the invitation that the General Conference already gave to us two years ago." So his dedicated mind could be at ease. Perhaps it would turn out to be right to take a furlough very soon. He smiled and drifted off into a dreamless sleep.

First Furlough

Frank and Florence lay on their travel cots at the end of the boxcar. The warm breezes of that early summer of 1919 whipped in through the open doors on either side, while the wheels below beat out a hypnotic, clacking rhythm on the rails.

"It's furlough time, Floss!" Frank reached for her hand. A smile lit up his pale, too-thin features. "We're on our way."

"Yes, sweetheart." Florence closed her eyes. Rest, change, no one sick—and the homeland just ahead in a few weeks. Ten years had been a long, long time. "It's good—very, *very* good. And weren't all those Indian soldiers kind to help us fix up this boxcar? A real rolling hotel!"

Excitement had swept through the Oster household when permission had been granted for them to join a northbound troop train of Indian soldiers. A whole boxcar just for them had been annexed at Tabriz. Even one-year-old Francis had caught the fever of joy. He spent the hours transfixed, watching the wild, majestic Russian Alps hurtle past the car doors. And when this show wearied the boys, Winton played castles, climbing over the packing boxes and swinging in their hammocks slung across the end of the car, keeping up a lively rhythm with the swaying of the train—all for little brother's entertainment. When Anna Benjamin wasn't busy cooking or washing, she always had time to play with them.

Anna's father was a Protestant minister in Urmia. When he learned that the Osters were leaving for America, he'd come to Frank with an urgent appeal. "Our son in America has sent money for Anna's passage." Tears had sprung to the man's eyes. "Perhaps we cannot see her again, but—because of conditions here, it is for the best, and we feel it's God's will. Would you?" The voice trailed off into uncertainty.

"Of course, my friend," Frank laid a reassuring hand on Pastor Benjamin's shoulder. "My wife and I will be glad to take Anna with us to New York. That's what you're asking, isn't it?"

"Oh, yes. You are very good, Mr. Oster. With you, I know she will be safe."

And so it was that the bright little teenager became one of the family for the homeward journey. Now Florence could relax and get the full benefit of a vacation, odd as the circumstances might be. Anna watched over the two little boys like a mother hen, and Frank and Florence could rest and doze off for two hours and more at a time. The rigors of famine-ridden Tabriz, the weeks and months of sickness, the innumerable round-the-clock missionary duties slowly dropped behind, and a sense of peace and healing settled over the creaking old boxcar.

The slow progress of the train toward the borders of Europe made the transition an entertaining and deliberate one. Because the eighty miles of railroad from Tabriz to Julfa had lain unused during the war years, there were frequent stops to repair bridges before the train could cross. Other scenic stops in wooded valleys were made when the men in the troop cars disembarked to cut down trees to feed the hungry steam engine. Time here was not, after all, "of the essence." At any rate, the train always waited while the men built campfires to cook their food.

During one of these stops, Frank sat in the boxcar doorway while Florence and Anna boiled potatoes on the small brazier standing in the corner. "I'm glad I don't have to get out and cut down a tree every time we want to eat," he smiled.

"After your illness, dear," Florence said, "we couldn't expect that, whether we got any food cooked or not." She bent to blow the coals in the brazier into a hot glow. "How fortunate we were to get a whole sack of coal in Tabriz! And the stack of *lavash* and bag of potatoes should see us all the way to Batumi, if we're careful."

At night the whole train lay like a great wooden snake curled up in some mountain gorge, fast asleep until sunrise. Then off it would crawl again. After many days the Osters, aboard their private observation boxcar, arrived in Batumi where they transferred to the ship that would take them through the narrow Bosporus Straits separating Europe from Asia.

The ocean voyage was a continuation of the leisurely train journey, punctuated by a series of port stops which astonished Anna. In Istanbul the Osters spent time ashore with the handful of church members who had survived the desert death marches of the war.

"Did you know all those people before?" Anna asked, as they returned to the ship from a pleasant evening of visiting around the *samovar.*

"Well, not exactly," Florence replied, "but they are Adventists, and we call them brothers and sisters. And, of course, one is always at home with brothers and sisters."

Anna looked at her with puzzled, wide, dark eyes. "You and Mr. Oster are the only missionaries I've ever seen—and your people receive you with open arms *everywhere,* as if you were really just one family. I don't understand."

"Well, it *is* one family," Florence explained. "When you belong to God's family, it doesn't matter whether we have actually seen each other before or not. If Jesus is the elder brother of all of us, then we have to be related, don't we?"

"Yes, I believe I understand," Anna reached automatically for Winton's hand as they headed up the steep slope of the gangplank onto their ship. "It must be a very nice family to belong to."

"It is, indeed," Florence answered, wondering if ever Anna might be claimed as a daughter of that family too. For the weeks that the girl would spend with the Oster family anyway, Florence prayed she would not see or hear anything to disillusion her about the "nice family" about which she had inquired.

A calm crossing of the Sea of Marmara and through the Dardanelles into the Aegean Sea ended in Piraeus, the harbor city of Athens. The rugged Greek countryside and the clear sunny air enchanted Florence. "Frank, I'd love to go swimming!" They were standing on the deck watching the fishing boats nuzzling the pier and the sunburned children swimming under the wharf supports. "The water's so clear! You can see thirty feet down, at least."

The many bathers on a nearby stretch of sand seemed to support her desire. "All right, Floss, why don't you go. It'll do you good."

"But wouldn't you go with me?"

"No, not now. I'll just stay up here with the baby. I don't feel quite up to it. Try me again another time." Frank smiled at her and gave her a little shove. "Go on. Have fun."

The sun and beach were all that the first view of them had promised, and Florence swam through the gentle swells with the abandon of a teenager. She hadn't felt so young and school-girlish since—well, she couldn't remember when. Anna was on the pier watching Winton, who was playing on the steps, fascinated with the barnacles that refused to be picked off the stones.

Some time later, tired and having had her fill, Florence left the water and dripped her way across the platform to the dressing room. She had no more than closed the splintery door when she heard a scream, "*Ah, vay!* [Oh dear!]" Wrenching the door open again, she saw Anna on the last step, hands clapped to her head. "*Ay vay! Ay, vay!*" The crescendo of shrieks froze Florence to the spot. Winton was nowhere to be seen.

Then, in a single involuntary, instinctive movement prompted neither by thought nor any conscious consideration, Florence darted across the pier and dived into the shady green water by the steps. In an instant she found the little boy, thrashing his way upward toward the hazy surface above. She seized him, threw him over one shoulder and kicked her way up to sun and air. Holding his head above water, she swam, one-armed, toward the pier steps.

Anna, in a paroxysm of fright, talked incessantly, still screaming at intervals, "Oh, Mrs. Oster, I watched him every minute. It happened fast. The slimy green seaweed there. He just slipped and went down so quickly. My hand almost touched him. *Ay VAY!* Oh, Mrs. Oster!"

Florence fought for her son's life, murmuring reassurances to Anna at the same time. She stretched Winton across her knees, face down, slapping his back. Then with a choke and a gurgle, a rush of water came out of the child, followed by a long cry which rivaled that of the distraught Anna. "My precious baby! Thank God!" Florence laid the little boy in the arms of the trembling Anna.

"Do you still trust me?" Anna sobbed.

"Of course, I trust you. It was an accident, but God has saved him for us." Florence looked back as she turned again to the dressing room, "Don't cry any more, dear."

Once back in the cabin, Florence changed the now-drowsy Winton into dry clothes and put him on his bunk. When she had told Frank the whole story, her resourcefulness and courage suddenly all seemed to be drained away, and she threw herself into her husband's arms. "Oh, Frank, we already have one little grave in Maragha. What if we should have had another one here in Athens!" She sobbed for a long while.

Frank smoothed her dark hair quietly, and waited until she had almost finished. "It's all right to cry, my darling." Then he tilted her chin up and looked into her eyes. "God has been very good to us once more. Remember our prayer about His will being done? He's answered now before we even had time to pray it."

Together they knelt by the berth to thank and praise once more the God of unspoken prayers.

The Mediterranean crossing passed almost without incident. Florence welcomed the calm, for the episode in Athens was not one from which she recovered rapidly. By the time the ship reached Marseille, France, however, her spirits were considerably restored.

"Frank, you went ashore the last time while we stayed on the ship. Now I'd like to do some sightseeing here."

Frank laughed. "Why, Floss, my trip into Naples was only a dull business affair. I can't see that it was anything to be coveted!"

"Maybe not," Florence replied, "but I just fancy going out to see Marseille. And the children have been cooped up on the boat for so long. I think they'd enjoy an outing too."

"All right, why don't you and Anna take the boys and go out on the town. I have a book I want to finish today, so I think I'll just stay by the ship, if you don't mind."

As the sightseeing party descended the gangplank, Frank called down from the upper deck. "Just don't forget that we sail at four o'clock this afternoon."

Florence looked up and laughed, "Oh, Frank! As if I'd forget a thing like *that!*"

Half a block from the dock area, they found a jolly, bewhiskered street merchant. His cart contained all kinds of marvels. "Come and buy," he called to them.

Winton already had his nose pressed up to the glass window in the side of the wagon, so the invitation was quite superfluous. The man spoke English! Florence rejoiced over this opportune discovery while she bought a pair of bird whistles for Winton and a rubber horse for Francis.

"We have only a few hours. What place is interesting to see in Marseille?" she inquired.

"Ah, madame, our city is *très belle*. The man pointed in a grand sweeping gesture to a distant hill beyond the edge of town. "Notre Dame de la Garde! All people coming take the cable car and go to the top." The man's moustache twitched with enthusiasm. "From there you can see *every*ting. Marseille, the bay, the harbor—*everyting!*"

Florence looked up at the fort and basilica atop the mountain. It would be a magnificent view.

"Yes, madame," the merchant pressed, "you will go? I will arrange."

"Yes, monsieur, we will go." Florence smiled at the man as he trotted off as fast as his age and bulk permitted, returning soon with a smart carriage driven by a fine-looking driver and a sleek pony wearing a little feather duster atop his head.

"The driver is very handsome, is he not?" Anna whispered in Florence's ear.

Florence studied the well-proportioned physique, the coal-black hair, the graceful swing as the young man leaped down from his seat to open the door for them. "Yes, Anna, you're right. He is certainly very handsome." Turning to the vendor she said, "Now be sure to arrange carefully with the driver. He must take us to the foot of the hill where we'll take the cable car. Then he must also be waiting there when we return so that he can drive us back to the ship which leaves at four o'clock this afternoon. Do you understand?"

"*Oui, oui,* Madame" the vendor flung his arms wide in a chivalrous gesture. "All is well. I have arranged all."

The carriage rattled along between rows of restaurants and curio shops, the horse's feather duster bobbing between his ears in a sprightly jig. At the cablecar terminal the driver bought their tickets and presented them with a flourish. One for going up—he pointed into the sunny blue French skies. The other for coming down—he indicated the worn pavement under his shiny leather boots. Speech was impossible, but Florence felt confident as the driver tied the horse to a hitching post and sauntered over to a sidewalk cafe. Their return to the ship would be assured.

The scenic ride up the mountain was well worth the effort. The city, green fields, and darker green forests beyond; the Mediterranean fading into a blue haze—it was as the man with the moustache had said. You could see "*every*ting." Anna, to say nothing of the boys, was delighted with the steep cable ascent and descent, and they all chattered over the novelty of it all. Florence smiled to herself. It had been worth the effort to bring the little boys off the ship for a few hours.

By 2:30 p.m. they were back at the bottom of the hill. But the carriage, the driver, and the horse—alas, they were gone. Even the feather duster. People on every side, but an impenetrable language barrier isolated Florence as much as if she had been left alone atop Mount Ararat. One after another, she stopped passersby, hoping for one glimmer of understanding and one syllable of advice as to how to get back to the harbor. The response was uniform and consistently French—a shrug of the shoulders, an apologetic flutter of the hands, an arch of the eyebrows, and they were gone—one and all. As nearly as Florence could ascertain, not a single word of English was known in all the dozens of shops clustered around the cable-car base.

"We're lost! We're lost! Anna cried.

Sensing the tension of the situation, both little boys raised their voices in long wails. Tears sprang to Florence's eyes too, but she forced them back, took out her handkerchief, and blew her nose instead. She looked at her watch. Only an hour left now until sailing time. What was to be done?

Down at the end of the block a gendarme appeared. She ran to meet him. Yes, to put oneself in the hands of the police—surely that would help. For the fifteenth or fiftieth time—she hardly knew which—she described their predicament. "Monsieur, we are lost. We must reach the dock. We don't know which—"

The policeman began to exhibit the same familiar mannerisms. He shrugged his shoulders; he waved his hands about; his eyebrows shot up as he murmured soft, unintelligible French phrases. He was just about to walk off when Florence grabbed him by the sleeve, hanging on in a desperation born of terror. What would she do in a foreign land without money, without passports, and without friends? The "nice family" which had so impressed

Anna—no, she couldn't be sure of finding one Adventist in this whole city. The gendarme seemed to be a last hope, and she couldn't let him go. Later she would remember the episode and laugh over it, as she recalled herself displaying some of the traits of the importunate widow described in the Bible story. But now it was 3:15 p.m., and as yet she hadn't made a single breakthrough.

Still hanging onto his arm, Florence worked herself around to stand in front of him. She pointed to the weeping children. "We go America on *S.S. President Wilson.*" She articulated every syllable with slow precision.

Again the policeman shrugged, as if to say, "Yes, I know President Wilson is in America, but what's that to me?"

Then, seized with an idea, Florence held up a finger. "Wait!" She rummaged in her purse and found a pencil and an old envelope. Quickly sketching a boat and writing the words *President Wilson* in large letters on the side, she said, "There!" Pointing again to the children she added, "We go on this boat. Toot, toot, toot to America." She penciled in a great volume of black smoke and tapped her watch crystal urgently.

Light dawned, as a flash from heaven. Smiling down on them benevolently, the policeman led them to the streetcar lines, spoke a few unknown words to the conductor and with a courteous smile bowed as he helped them on to the car.

All was well, until fifteen minutes later when the conductor ordered them off. Knowing they were still miles from the wharf, Florence refused to move. The man insisted. Amid waving arms and a thorough mixture of French persuasion and English protest, they all disembarked. The conductor aligned them on the curbside, and they were made to realize that they were to wait for the next streetcar. When it came, they boarded it wholly by faith, not sight. They were presently rewarded by the sight of the docks.

At last! There was their ship, smoke belching from all the funnels, even as Florence had demonstrated it to the gendarme. They found Frank pacing the deck. "Well, thank God, you're here!" Frank had clearly been anxious. "Where *have* you been?" He pulled out his watch as he must have done a dozen times in the past hour. "I was about to get up a search party."

"It's a long story, Frank." Florence sighed. "Let's go to our cabin, and I'll tell you there."

The family threaded its way down the narrow passage. "I can't understand, Mrs. Oster, why that carriage driver would do such a thing," Anna said. "And he was so smart and handsome too."

Florence felt almost too weary to smile at Anna's naiveté, but she had to anyway. "Well, Anna, you'll find that good looks often have very little to do with kindness. But, of course, we must remember that perhaps there really was a misunderstanding, and he didn't realize that he should wait for us."

The ship anchored at Gibraltar the next day. "Floss, would you like to go sightseeing in Gibraltar and Algiers today? I understand that a party from the ship plans to go over to the African side this afternoon."

"Oh no! No thanks."

Then Florence heard an almost simultaneous echo of her words from Anna. "Oh, Mr. Oster, No! Let's just stay here and watch from the ship. That will be enough."

After the adventures in Marseille the family unanimously agreed that staying aboard would indeed "be enough."

The Atlantic crossing culminated in that final scene which has been familiar to many generations of missionaries, long years away from home. The Statue of Liberty ushered ships in past her feet and on to the docks, where ships blended with shore, and passengers moved off somewhere into the New York skyline—the gateway to America.

Anna's every breath was a gasp of astonishment. The skyscrapers with sunless street "gorges" between them. The cars—it seemed she would never get over the cars. In between her cries of wonder and the clearing of their luggage through customs, the Osters somehow got to the Times Square Hotel and managed, at the same time, to savor for themselves some of the deep feelings that came with setting foot once more on their homeland.

Anna had a room on the floor above, in the hotel, and Florence made sure that she got safely to bed. The large porcelain bathtub with hot and cold running water preoccupied the girl for half an hour at least. "Yes, it's quite different," Florence agreed, "from the shallow bathing pans in Persia." As she was leaving for her own room, she pointed to the gas lamp on the side table. "When you want to turn out the light, you just turn this little knob, see?"

"Yes, Mrs. Oster," Anna replied from the bathroom, where she was still experimenting with hot and cold water mixtures.

Later, after they had celebrated their first bedtime worship together in the homeland, Frank and Florence were well ready for sleep. Then a sudden urgent pounding on their door jerked them back to reality as fear clutched at Florence's heart.

The hotel desk clerk stood in the hall. "Come upstairs, quickly!" he said. "Your friend has tried to gas herself."

"What! Anna?"

"Yes, the girl. When she ignored our knock, we unlocked the door and went in and turned off the gas."

Florence threw on her bathrobe and rushed up to Anna's room. There under a shaking bundle of bedding, quilts pulled up over her head, lay a tearful Anna. "Oh—oh—oh, Mrs. Oster! Those men!" The girl reached up and pulled Florence down and buried her face in her shoulder. "It was bad enough to experience those Persian massacres. But here I was with the door securely locked, and those men forced their way in—" With huge, terrified eyes she peered at the imposters in the doorway.

"There, there, Anna. Those men saved your life." Florence soothed. "Couldn't you smell the gas?"

"No," Anna sniffed and sobbed uncontrollably. "I blew and blew real hard, until the light went out."

"I'm so thankful," Florence sighed with relief. "They smelled the poisonous gas escaping under your door, and they came in time to save you." Then she nodded to the men, who closed the door and left her alone with the girl. "Tell me, dear, did you have a good bath?"

"How could I? The water ran out as fast as it came in. What could I do?"

"Oh, I'm sorry. I forgot to show you how to use the stopper." Florence had a fleeting memory of herself, a young bride, learning the ways of Iran. Yes, Anna would have many things to discover. "Let's sleep now, Anna."

The next morning Anna's brother, a young Presbyterian clergyman, arrived. She rushed into his arms and they wept together. Finally he pulled out his handkerchief and wiped their eyes. "Now we'll forget all the sad things of the past. We have each other in this new land."

Standing back, he surveyed his sister more critically. Her fresh young beauty was not really diminished by her worn, shapeless dress, but it didn't attract the kind of attention her brother wanted for her. He pulled out his wallet and handed it to Florence. "There, take Anna to Wanamakers store and buy her a complete wardrobe of new clothes. I want my lovely sister to feel perfectly at home in her new country."

Florence knew that Anna had found her family, but she paused to offer up another small prayer that both of them would always remain part of God's great family too.

Now the Osters took up the more personal part of their homecoming. A visit to the General Conference headquarters in Washington, D.C. reminded them of what they had always known—that they were part of the vanguard of the church organization. Florence remembered hard, lonely days over the years when they had longed for just such reassurance. Physical examinations at the Washington Sanitarium found them to be in relatively good condition, all things considered. Nurses came from all over the building to see how thin Winton and Francis were—shoulder blades and ribs all projecting. Florence remembered ruefully that she had weighed 145 pounds when she went to Persia, but now she could barely tip the scale to 90.

Then came the transcontinental train journey to Washington state. Home again.

The months of furlough passed, as all furloughs should, in resting and in visiting friends and family. At no time, however, did they forget that Persia was really home. That night long ago when Florence had reminded Frank as he convalesced from typhus that "our hearts are always here no matter where else we might ever be," had been a commitment from which nothing in America could wean them. With mounting anticipation they looked forward to returning to Persia.

And then the General Conference informed them that no visas were available because of "civil strife and war with Russia." How familiar that sounded, and it brought a host of vivid scenes to mind. They needed no imagination to know what was going on there—the famine, the Kurds, the violence, and the epidemics.

So they had to wait, but it turned out to be a pleasant detour. Frank was ordained to the ministry at his *alma mater*, Walla Walla College, and given the pastorship of the Hood River Church in

Oregon. To his pastoral duties Frank added much travel—to camp meetings, high schools, and civic clubs. While he brought new members into his congregation, he also raised funds for the Near East Relief Foundation. Though Azerbaijan was half a world away, Frank and Florence were almost as much a part of it as if they had been there in person, distributing *lavash* and nursing refugees in their living room. The responsibility never left their minds.

Of course, pastoral and public service; closeness with Vandella and other relatives; inexhaustible supplies of Hood River apples to eat; and then the birth of another son, Kenneth—all these things kept life rich and interesting. Still, life remained partially unfulfilled, and they went on waiting for those Persian visas to come through.

Shadows of the Russian Revolution

When departure time finally came, spring had already arrived in the Pacific Northwest. It was 1922. Farewells now replaced the former welcomes. Then the train journey to New York and the voyage to Istanbul completely retraced their homecoming trip of almost two years earlier.

That first furlough trip, although not without adventure, had been benignly uneventful compared to the avalanche of problems which was to beset the family at the end of this return trip. On the first night at sea after leaving Istanbul, Francis complained, "My head hurts, Mommy." By midnight he was vomiting and burning with high fever. Thereafter, his night fevers were constant.

On the afternoon of May twenty-first, the ship reached Batumi, Russia. For unexplained reasons, passengers were not allowed to disembark, so Francis had to be nursed through another night-fever in the cramped cabin.

In the morning, officials on the dock took the Oster's passports and then hustled the family off to prison without a word of explanation. The whole day passed. "Surely, we'll be released by nightfall," Florence said. "What in the world can they mean by doing this to us."

"I don't know," Frank replied, "but we seem to have hit another delay in God's time clock. We can only wait and see. I discovered that today is their national independence day here for their new Soviet state of Georgia. Perhaps that has something to do with anti-foreign feelings, or something."

"But you're on a Swiss passport, and that—"

"Yes, I know." Frank, as usual, could see the practical side. "But even the Swiss are foreign too in the last analysis, no matter how middle-of-the-road they may appear most of the time."

"Well, it seems that we're here for the night," Florence admitted. "We'll have to make the best of it until morning."

No food had been provided all day, and there were no chairs. The twenty men in the room had found sleeping places here and there, under the noses of the many guards with drawn bayonets stationed inside and outside of the doors. Florence made a bed for five-year-old Winton on the floor, and five-month-old baby Kenneth, all unaware, dropped off to sleep in his go-cart.

Francis cried with the pains in his stomach, and nothing could relieve the misery of the three-year-old. Frank approached a guard. "This child has been sick for days. Please allow us to have a cot for him."

"*Nyet!*" was the reply, and neither Frank nor Florence had strength to argue the point. She made him a bed too on the dirty floor beside Winton.

"At first, I thought we were fortunate to get that army doctor to look at Francis this afternoon. But now this prescription he gave us—" Florence looked at the scrap of paper stuck into the outer pocket of her purse. "What's the use, if we can't get it filled anyway? And on top of that, we know there's a train leaving for Tiflis tonight. And," she added darkly, "we were supposed to be on it too."

"Come, come, Floss, try to lie down and rest a little. You're too tired." Frank took his Bible out of his bag. "We need to read Romans 8:28 again, and then pray our prayer. God must know why we're in prison. Things will be better in the morning, surely."

And so the prisoners slept—even Francis, restless in his discomfort. But not Florence. She stayed up, sitting in an abandoned steamer chair and writing a letter to her mother, feeling very much a little girl in need of her homefolks. The long night hours were punctuated by several toilet trips with Francis, each time with an escort of guards with bayonets fixed on them.

At dawn four soldiers with long bayonets on their guns escorted Frank from the prison cell. As soon as he was out of sight, the Swiss consul, who was a fellow prisoner, approached Florence as she was getting the last remnants of food out of the lunch basket to give the children. "I'm very sorry to say it, lady, but you should know that you'll probably never see your husband again. Don't you hear the shooting outside even now?"

Stark terror seized Florence's mind. "Do you mean that?" She fought with the words.

The older man looked at her kindly. "Yes, I've seen too many go already. Don't ever expect him to come back."

Florence felt numb. She then began to turn the situation over in her mind. They had been through so much. Was it all going to end this way? Then, it came to her. There was, of course, only one place to go. "Come, Winton, we're going to pray now for Daddy. Let's kneel down here by Francis' bed."

"Where did Daddy go?" Winton studied his mother's face gravely.

"He went outside, and he may be in great danger. We must ask Jesus to take care of him."

Two simple prayers went up, and to hers Florence added the phrase, "Thy will be done." It was still a struggle to say those words, but as one crisis had succeeded another, she had found a growing peace and contentment following each act of submission on her part.

Meanwhile, Frank was being cross-examined by the *checka*—the forerunner of the NVD, or Secret Service. The questions seemed foolish: "What is the name of your king?" "How old is he?" "Does he have many servants?" "Do you like traveling in Russia?" "Can your wife cook good borsch (soup)?" "Do you prefer to ride in a carriage or on a bicycle?"

True, these inexperienced new officers of the *checka* were not asking any questions that would be of significant value to the Secret Service. But nonetheless they had power, even if they weren't sure what to do with it, and all prisoners were being treated as spies until they were proved innocent. So, in these extended interrogations, Frank seriously and carefully answered each question. Had he been in the skilled hands of the former officers of the Czarist regime, matters might have been quite different.

The haphazard questioning ended when none of the *checka* could think of anything else to talk about, and Frank was returned to the prison under guard. The iron gate clanked open and he walked in. Winton flew into his arms with Florence close behind.

"Oh, Frank. You are alive! You are here!" Nothing else mattered now.

"I'm very glad that I was wrong, Mrs. Oster." The low voice came from the consul, leaning against the wall under the window. "Very glad."

About an hour later another officer opened the prison door, and with a wide sweep of his arm motioned the Osters out toward the street and freedom. *"Prejalsta,* [If you please]," he said. But his courtesy ended right there. They had to find their own way to the train station and wait their turn to go through customs. Just how their liberation had been brought about was not known until they later met Mr. Ekkerman of the Near East Relief Foundation. He had asked an officer-friend why the Osters were imprisoned. No one, as it turned out, knew why. So they had been released within the hour.

"I certainly have reason now," Frank mused, "to be grateful for all those hours I spent fund-raising for the Near East Relief Foundation."

Watching others go through customs at the train station became increasingly disquieting to Frank and Florence. In their search for hidden documents, the officers ripped out coat linings, and some suitcases were literally dismembered. "My!" Florence exclaimed, "we have eighteen pieces of luggage. What's going to become of it all?"

"We'd better prepare ourselves to lose a good deal of it," Frank replied, "but there's something else that worries me."

"What?"

"You remember that piece of paper we took off our door in Tabriz after the Kurdish massacres? The one that said 'No Christians to Live?' What if they find *that?*"

"Where is it?" Florence remembered how Frank had shown that paper in camp-meeting talks. It had made events very real to the people who heard his stories.

"In the inner pocket of the Gladstone bag," Frank whispered. "I don't know what they'd make of that if they found it."

Well, that again was something that God would have to take in charge. But no customs call came that day. Nor the next, nor the one after.

Meanwhile, they relocated their possessions, and found lodging the first night in an unventilated little room in a houseful of refugees, bedbugs, and fleas. Florence had been hungry for so long, and she had begun to dream, of apple pies made of Hood River apples. The family supper they were served, however, was almost airborne with flies, and so she tried to stop thinking about food at all.

The next day Frank found a room in a cleaner part of town where they enjoyed the luxury of three beds—one with springs, one with boards, and one with canvas. They used coats for mattresses, their clothes for pillows, and the rugs for covers. Once settled, they called in another doctor for Francis. He studied the three-year-old's thin little body, took his temperature, and decided it must be either typhoid or malaria.

"Do you think he should continue on the milk diet he's had since he first became ill?" Florence inquired.

"Well, yes, I think that's a good idea," the doctor said. "Here are some powders to put in his milk. They should bring his fever down."

With this rather sketchy medical attention, they had to turn their thoughts to getting through customs. Dutifully they unpacked and repacked everything they owned, toiling under the eyes of the impassive officer.

At last the officer said, "It is finished."

Stunned, Florence and Frank hurried out of the station. Nothing had been confiscated, and no tax had been charged!

"Unbelievable!" Frank said. "Let's hurry on our way before anyone changes his mind."

Of course, there couldn't be anything so simple as just going and getting on the train. They were still detained. Frank had to report to the police daily, but on the credit side of the ledger, Francis finally got well and Kenneth cut two teeth. Twenty-one days they had stayed in Batumi.

One morning, coming from his police visit, Frank announced, "We're allowed to leave today."

Florence felt exuberant. At last! No matter what else might happen they would be moving. Just to be going somewhere was in itself exhilaration. A few hours later, after she had settled the boys down for the journey, she relaxed in her seat and let the rhythmic click of the wheels lull her to sleep.

As the train squealed to a stop at the first station, Florence jerked up out of a sound sleep. When an armed guard appeared at the door of their compartment, she froze into terrified wakefulness.

"Mr. Oster, you must report to the police in this town." The guard clicked his heels and waited for Frank to follow him.

Soon the Osters discovered that this was to be a regularly scheduled event at every town they would pass through. "It'll be all right, Floss. Just routine exercise for me. And I *have* had a lot of practice already, you know," Frank said.

One delay en route south which did not vex Frank and Florence was a one-week stopover in a small town in the Caucasus Mountains. Despite the daily trip to the police station, they could thoroughly enjoy the time with Mr. and Mrs. Sperling. The Sperlings were the first converts won by Henry Dirksen and Frank back in 1911. When the war had started in 1914, they'd left Urmia and returned home to Russia. A talented musician, Sperling had become the conductor of the city orchestra of Erivan. Now the Sperling's son and daughter had also joined the Adventist church.

Over the ever-present samovar, the two couples spent memorable hours reviewing the many years that had separated them. "The Bolsheviks came," Brother Sperling said, "but I stayed. After all, this is now home. How can one be forever a refugee?"

"And how did you manage? Did your music help?" Frank asked.

"Yes and no. The Bolsheviks here loved music—the best classics, you know. I played for them, and all was well. Except that trouble came later because of it."

"How was that?" Florence thought she had become accustomed to the ebb and flow of fortune in this stressful world of the Near East, but events always were taking odd turns.

"When the Armenians returned to the city," Sperling went on, "I was arrested because I had played for the Bolsheviks. That Captain Vagharshak—he's a fiery one. He threatened to kill me."

"What did you say?"

"What could I say? I had played. I couldn't deny that." The musician shrugged. "I told him that the baker is also obliged to bake for all, regardless of what they believe."

"And then he let you go?" Florence remembered again how the cool, casual, off-hand stance is often one's best defense. It had worked for Frank and her too, and not that many days ago, either.

"Yes, he dismissed me—after I had played the Armenian

national air for him on my violin," Sperling smiled. " 'You're also one of us,' he said then." He leaned back and crossed his legs, fully relaxed. "It is as I have always said—music is for use, not just pleasure."

Mrs. Sperling leaned forward to set her cup on the table. "And our two children also had a very great test too. And so young—only seven and nine years old at the time."

Florence looked at their hostess, arrested by the catch in her voice. "What happened?"

"Ach! It was that street sweeper. I know he was the one," she exclaimed with heat.

Mr. Sperling nodded. "Yes, undoubtedly he was the one. Creeping along by the houses, listening to whoever might be saying the word *God*."

"And then?" Frank leaned forward, gazing intently at the speaker.

"Well, all the children were taken to the City Hall, early in the morning, and—"

"And they had nothing to eat *all* day," Mrs. Sperling's hand trembled as she took up her empty cup again. The memory of the ordeal clearly came over her again. "Do you know what the officers said?"

"What?" Florence's mind took in the whole pitiful scene and her eyes began to smart with unshed tears.

"They told them, 'Now pray to your God for food!' And they kept at them for hours, 'Pray harder—Don't you believe your God can help?—See, it's no use!' "

"And what happened?" Frank asked.

"Nothing," Sperling replied. "Nothing at all. Then they said, 'Now pray to Stalin for food.' "

"So the children prayed again," his wife went on.

"Poor little lambs!" Florence felt a rising suspicion as to how the story would end.

"And after that the men flung open the doors of the banquet hall. The tables were loaded with food. 'See, your God doesn't do anything. This is what Stalin gives you.' "

"Oh, dear friends!" Florence could see the hungry children devouring the dreadful feast. "How could you ever persuade a child against such an argument as that?"

"We couldn't, of course," Mr. Sperling said simply. "Only the Spirit of God could eventually erase the results of that experience."

"So now, you see," the mother concluded, "why we are so very thankful that both our son and daughter have now joined us in the church. A victory, truly."

Days later, the Osters reached Tiflis. The Adventist pastor whom they had met on their first entry to Persia many years earlier met them. Because of his wife's illness, he explained to them in German that he couldn't take them to his home; but they could put up their travel cots in his little chapel. He would do his best to help them with meals.

The wife's illness, they soon discovered, was mental. On first sight she shook her fists at them and tried to hit Frank over the head with a chair. The pastor explained that he was away from home during the Revolution, and his wife was sure he was dead. When he suddenly showed up again, her mind gave way. Now she wouldn't let him out of her sight and was insanely jealous whenever he spoke to other people. The Osters had to stay for another twelve days in Tiflis under these seemingly unbearable circumstances, while Frank, of course, reported daily to the police. When their southward journey resumed, they were questioned at every town and often detained for days at a time. Thus the two-day trip stretched into nine weeks. As Florence looked out on the lovely mountain scenery, she recalled their northward journey at the beginning of their furlough and longed for the leisure and privacy of their old boxcar.

Arrival in Julfa brought them at last within sight of Persia, just across the Arāks River. Another eighty miles to go, and they would be in Tabriz—at *home!* The Bolshevists, however, had more interrogations for them. These stretched on for days.

At last Frank came back to the hotel to say that they were about to move again. "I think we'll be going through customs tomorrow, Floss." He drew her close to him. "Cheer up, sweetheart. Persia's just across the river now."

"Just over the river. And then we'll be through with all the unrest of this Russian Revolution, won't we?" Florence wondered at times how many more lessons in extreme patience they would be required to learn before they could "graduate" into a routine life—as routine, at least, as theirs was ever going to be.

"There's something else too, Floss," Frank went on. "I heard it whispered among the travelers that a very thorough search will be made. All money, valuables, and who knows what will be taken from us."

"What are we going to do then, Frank? You know we need every bit of money we've got left for our fares to Tabriz."

"I've got an idea." Frank always had an idea, and Florence smiled as he walked over to the window and pulled the shades down as tightly as possible. From the lunch box he took out a can of evaporated milk, opened it and poured the contents into a bowl. In the bottom of the empty can he carefully placed their three remaining five-dollar gold pieces. Next he sealed them in with melted candle wax, and replaced some of the milk. He turned down the cover and put the milk can back into the lunch basket. "There! Now let's drink the rest of the milk—to celebrate what's going to be a success!"

"Frank, you're so resourceful. No wonder you ended up with pioneering to do." Florence felt proud of him. He would outwit anyone in the *checka,* for sure.

The next morning they presented themselves at customs. Six-year-old Winton was entrusted with the lunch basket while Frank and Florence attended to the more important luggage. Frank underwent a search in one room and Florence in another. Every article of clothing had to be removed and inspected by the officers. During the baggage search which followed, every book, paper, and diary they had was confiscated. When they were finally dismissed they went outdoors, light in heart. "Come, Winton," Frank took the boy's free hand in his. "We'll stop and have some lunch."

Arrival on the other side of the river brought its own kind of drama. The passengers had lost most of their possessions at the border, but now they were *home.* Many flung themselves down onto the good Persian earth and kissed it. "Allah be praised, for He is merciful," they cried. Then they arose, and in a last, grand gesture spat toward Russia on the other side of the river.

On the train to Tabriz at last, the Osters reviewed the long, long journey. "To think we lost our notes and papers in Julfa, Frank," Florence sighed.

"I know, Floss. But it was, after all, only paper. We have our lives, and," he added, "we still have some money."

"Yes, Frank, but all those journals I've kept through the years. From them I was one day going to write a book about our work in Persia, as so many of our friends have suggested." Her voice trailed off in discouragement.

"I know, darling. But God perhaps has some other way of getting the story written, if He wants it done. Meanwhile, you and I shall just go on living it now." Frank pointed out the window to a *caravansary* they both knew well. "See, Floss, we're nearing home again."

Just a few miles further down the track, however, the train stopped out in the open country. The guard came through the cars announcing the delay. "The Kurds are attacking the next village through which we must pass. We'll continue in the morning." So they bedded down in the railway car for the night.

The last stage of the journey was completed in safety, ending five whole months of travel. "Do you know, Frank, that we've unpacked and repacked all our luggage twenty-three times since we left Washington?" Florence exclaimed.

"I can believe it." Frank affirmed cheerfully.

They found Persia's national army battling insurgent Kurds again, and famine conditions still persisted. A letter from Mother White awaited them. Having been five months on the way, it reminded them of their isolation in both time and distance. She had just read of their arrest in Batumi six weeks previously and poured all her mother-anxiety into the letter. "We must write to her immediately and set her mind at rest," Florence said.

"We seem to be taking up life here just about where we left off before our long furlough," Frank remarked. "Business as usual every way we look. So, welcome to Persia, Floss—for the second time."

Barrier Breakthrough

The Osters found things not nearly as bad as they might have been after their absence of almost three years. Their household belongings, which had been stored in the basement of a friend's home, had remained exactly as they had left them, untouched by human hands. This fact seemed all the more remarkable when they learned that people had fled from the city twice, and that once soldiers had robbed the people in the streets and looted the houses throughout their district.

Florence regarded their collection of storage boxes with a sort of reverence. "They're nothing but our common everyday possessions," she told Frank, "but how good of God to take care of them for us. He knew how badly we needed them, right down to the last cup and towel."

Javaher, who had been widowed before the Oster's furlough, came to visit shortly after their return. She told about finding work with the Fassum family—American Lutheran missionaries. But then, in one swift raid, bandits had come into the town. They had killed Mr. Fassum; taken all the contents from the homes in Sāūjbulāgh; and then stripped the clothing from Mrs. Fassum, three other American women, and herself. They were then turned out into the street. Naked, the women escaped with the children to a neighboring village, where they begged for some *lavash* and collected some dirty rags to cover themselves.

"But we had yet another difficulty," Javaher went on. "My son Lazarus still had that overcoat you gave him two years before. The Kurds demanded it, and he refused."

"Dear me," Florence exclaimed. "I hope he gave it to them. I can easily make him another coat. What a time to argue about a coat!"

"No," Javaher replied. "For all that, he's fourteen years old already. He wept and said *Khanoom* Oster had made it for him and he would keep it. They put a gun to his heart and demanded the coat again."

"Poor Lazarus! To face death for that old coat!" Florence felt tears come to her eyes.

"I begged him to take it off. And finally he did. They took not only his coat but all his other clothes as well," Javaher shook her head as if to dislodge the terrifying scene from her mind. "But he cared only for the coat—the rest didn't matter."

"Thank God, the boy's life was spared." Florence arose to lead the way to the bedroom, where most of the packing boxes stood. "I just opened a trunk yesterday, and in it I think I have some material that will make Lazarus a new coat. Let's see."

The small, personal tragedy of Lazarus and his coat stood as only a pathetic sample of the chaotic conditions still existing on the public scene. One day Frank and Florence took the children with them to make a missionary call. On the way home, a great army parade blocked their way. It took some time for about 5000 infantry and cavalry—flanked by cannons, guns, spears, flags, and ammunition carts—to go by. One company of horsemen carried very long poles with murderous broad knives attached to the ends. A parade? Yes, but the multitude was, in fact, the army returning from a battle with the Kurds at Urmia. Still, a certain grandeur glamorized them, as they marched along chanting, "*Zindehbad* Iran! Iran *Aziz!* [Long live Iran! dear Iran!]." The victorious war song went on to describe how the enemy had been conquered and Ismail Agha, the Kurdish leader, had been put to flight. In the minds of the bystanders, Frank and Florence included, there still arose an anxious thought. Ismail Agha still lived. Would he not rally more troops and return to plunder and kill again?

The parade staggered the imaginations of Winton and Francis. For the rest of the day they bombarded their parents with questions. Winton was old enough to have figured out a few answers for himself, and Kenneth was still much too young to verbalize his ideas. But Francis, the four-year-old extrovert, needed answers to his questions. "How could God make so many soldiers and people?" "Where are they going?" "Where did they come from?" "Where do they eat?" "Where do they sleep?" Francis could hardly wait for the questions to be answered—the main thing seemed to be to get them *asked!*

While the Osters' work resumed immediately, upon their arrival back in Tabriz, getting settled into their home had to be delayed for several weeks. Missionary friends had rented a house for them, and they had had a comfortable place to stay from the first night of their arrival home. Their salary had increased, of course, beyond their initial weekly wage of nine dollars fifty cents as appointed by Elder Conradi some ten years before, but still it remained very modest. Disappointing as it was, they had to find a cheaper place to live.

The transition, and the temporary atmosphere which prevailed around the house, vexed Francis. The long journey from America, followed by continued living out of boxes, had been too much. One evening as he knelt to pray before going to bed, the child said, "Dear Jesus, if you please, have an officer fix up our home in heaven so we won't have to wait for it when we get there."

The day finally came for the move to the lesser house. Francis watched Florence pack up the kitchenware. With a sigh that bespoke his heavy weight of concern, he asked, "Do we need to pack up everything before we go to heaven?"

Florence stopped short in surprise, trying to hide her smile. "Why, Francis dear, we—"

But the little fellow's mind had already leaped ahead and found a solution. "Oh, I know what Jesus can do! He can send the angels to help us pack, can't He? And then they can help us unpack too when we get there."

"Jesus has an even better idea than that, Francis," Florence sat down on a box and drew him to her. "He has all new and beautiful things for us up there, and we won't need to take any of these old ones with us. Won't that be fine?"

When Francis' anxiety had been set at rest and he had trotted off to explain it all to Kenneth, Florence went back to the packing. The wagon would be at the door too soon, if she didn't hurry. But she couldn't help wondering if that all-time favorite text about the preparing of the "many mansions" in the Father's house didn't have a special meaning for missionaries and their children. Who else could understand so fully the marvel of having a home—and complete, without effort and stress.

Within six months of their return from furlough, the Osters' Sabbath School grew to over 130 members. Lesson study was conducted in three languages: Turkish, Syriac (Assyrian), and Armenian. Opportunities to work, pray, and preach increased. While growing attendance at the meetings brought great fulfillment, it also created problems on other levels.

The living room of the Oster's home overflowed with people, at every meeting. They even filled the halls. Every one came—rich and poor, great and small, citizens and refugees. And after every meeting fleas and lice overran the house. Florence waged a constant battle on the homefront. Quarantines were unknown, and every time a crowd gathered there were definite chances of being exposed to contagious diseases. Having nursed the three boys through measles and pinkeye, Florence could only pray daily that they would be spared diphtheria, smallpox, or something worse.

"Frank, let's find a different place for the crowd, other than the room we have to live in," she finally begged.

"Yes, Floss, I know the problem—and I'm working on it. Just give me a little more time, all right?"

Finally Frank found a substantial building which, when several walls had been knocked out, provided a very suitable meeting place. Moreover, the new location began to lend to the gatherings something of the status of a *church.* Within another six months the Bible studies had evolved into sermons, and then a Missionary Volunteer Society was added. The number of regular attendants at the meetings now reached 200.

On a Sabbath late in May, the second Seventh-day Adventist baptism was celebrated in Persia. The believers met by a stream in a lovely grove just outside the city. Florence watched Frank waiting in the pool of flowing water for the seventeen candidates to come down to him one by one. Behind his dignified, fine features she could read the deep feelings that the occasion stirred within him. To work twelve seemingly unproductive years to establish the first church had been a long time. But now some vast barrier seemed to have broken. For the past year it was not necessary for them to push the work. The work, indeed had been pushing *them,* far beyond their ability to perform.

Among the new members there stood Khoja Aziz, who had worked unceasingly among the thousands of Armenian and Syrian refugees who had fled to Tabriz. He had waited for eight years for this day, and now tears stood in his blind eyes. Then Captain Vagharshak—how fitting that he should be in the second baptism, for he was a natural link with the first, nine years ago. Florence remembered Frank's early letters from Urmia describing Brother Sperling, his wife, and their baptism. The captain, a great fighter and leader of Armenian troops, had threatened Brother Sperling with death because he had played music for the Bolshevists.

Few present had ever seen a baptismal service before, and the scene clearly impressed them. The charter members of the first Persian church were Frank and Florence, along with Mr. and Mrs. Ruben Joseph, who had been baptized earlier into the ancient Nestorian Church, and the seventeen new members. What the company may have lacked in numbers was made up for in quality, for not one member or Sabbath School attendant had come without threats of stoning and death. Even the school children had faced beating and other punishments every Monday morning.

Now, with a home-base church established, Frank could turn his attention to outlying villages, and calls came from all sides. After five years of exile in Tabriz, several came, on behalf of the thousands of Assyrians of the Nestorian Church, and begged Frank and Florence to return with them to their homes in Urmia and establish schools there. This was not possible, of course, for Florence had just opened her own little two-room school, so there could be little hope of opening a school anywhere else.

One day, however, Frank felt impressed to go to Urmia. "I feel that I should go, Floss," he said. "Who knows what those dear people face, going home after an absence of five years. At least I could hold meetings for a few weeks."

The weeks stretched into two months, in which Frank preached twice a day. Several doctors, teachers, and other professionals were won to Christ. These would form the nucleus of the Urmia Church. He came home with stories of the desperate plight of the refugees, who had returned to houses and vineyards that had been totally destroyed. Most found not so much as a single wall standing. Mid-winter had arrived, and children suffered frostbite, going to school through the snow with virtually no clothes on. Scarcely one pair of trousers could be seen that didn't have bare skin showing through. Underwear had become unknown, and one little girl turned up at a meeting with only one sleeve in her threadbare dress.

Relief work now consumed all the spare hours. Florence had not supposed that she *had* any spare time, but by the end of January she realized that somehow she must have had leisure hours after all. In that month, with the help of a couple of women from the church, she cut out and made twenty suits of clothes—undershirts, underpants, trousers, and Russian-style blouses for the boys; and shirts, panties, and dresses for the girls.

Meanwhile Frank kept up his missionary journeys—sometimes on horseback, sometimes with camel caravans, sometimes in carriages—always long and tiring. One day an urgent call came from a little out-of-the-way village. Because of the great need among the many Assyrian refugees, Frank included the place on one of his missionary itineraries. Since no inns were available, he accepted the hospitality of the Sangarloo family during his stay there.

Long after his return to Tabriz, he couldn't forget the bright-eyed attention he received during his Bible studies evening after evening, from seventeen-year-old Yoash, who always sat cross-legged on the bare ground at his feet. "I keep thinking about that boy, Floss," he said. "The Lord must have a special plan for him."

Months later, after the Kurdish raids tapered off, Frank met the Sangarloos again back home in Urmia. Yoash had been studying hard in a mission boarding school, but he hadn't forgotten Frank and the Bible studies.

Together they huddled under the *kursi* and talked. "The Assyrians, you say, aren't included in the prophecy of Daniel 2?" Yoash asked, his quick mind very much aware of his own ancient national origins.

"You must remember, of course," Frank said, "that Daniel didn't live until after the decline of Assyria. The prophecy starts with Babylon. Assyria and Nineveh had already passed into history."

The discussion went on—to Persia, very much alive and still present, and then to Greece and Rome. Yoash could see himself as playing an active, vital part in the drama of prophecy and history. Assyria, Babylon, Persia—these he could understand. And then came "a kingdom which shall never be destroyed." Again the teenager tried to identify personally with Daniel's prophecy. First Daniel had spoken of his ancestors, and now the call was for him—Yoash Sangarloo. Who could resist? Not he.

His response matched that of James and John, who had declared that they would ever "drink of the cup" Christ offered. His baptism called up a storm of scorn, abuse, and persecution from all sides; but his determination not to retaliate brought a quiet peace and confidence he had never felt before. His response gave him a strength that enabled him to face repeated tests on the question on final examinations on the Sabbath and to finally face expulsion from school because he was "a Jew."

Three years of study, and now he seemed to have lost all, with no hope of further education—a bitter disappointment for someone so much inclined to study. But he stood firm and waited to see what his God would do. And in September the principal called him back to school. "We're convinced you'll not give up your Jewish ideas," he said, "so we invite you back to school and promise to honor your religious convictions. And you may take your examinations privately on a weekday."

Military service posed the next challenge, for every Persian youth had to bear arms seven days a week during his time of service. The laws of the "Medes and Persians" were still not prone to change, and no leniency could be expected. But God had already marked his young man, and when Yoash went to register at the conscription office, he discovered that his age had been erroneously recorded as ten years above his actual age. (Ages were dated from "before" or "after" a Kurdish raid.) There it stood on the records—so he was rejected as being too old for service.

Yoash eventually became one of the first students at the new Seventh-day Adventist Worker Training School. Later he went on to serve as a minister in Persia until his retirement in 1968. Always close to the Oster family, it was not surprising that he should later choose to name his baby daughter "Florence" in honor of the one who became a second mother to him.

At the request of Mr. and Mrs. Niewert, formerly of the Tiflis

Church, Frank went to Engeli on the Caspian Sea. The northward journey entailed two weeks' travel by carriage in scorching mid-summer heat. When he reached Engeli, he found that Brother Niewert had been sent on a trip to Teheran by the Russian engineering firm which employed him. Frank opened his public meetings anyway and fought for every inch of ground. He preached in Turkish for the benefit of the local people. An interpreter with very limited abilities tried to translate into Russian for the foreigners.

One night after a meeting Frank found a note, written in Russian, lying on a corner table: "Because your preaching is undesirable in this community we will give you twenty-four hours to leave the city. If you fail to leave by that time, we will kill you." This was signed by a member of the anarchists, named Bullet.

Agitation swept through the little company. "Oh, you must leave at once. Your life is truly in danger," one person said.

"No, stay and report it to the authorities," another urged.

"Let's just leave it where it is," Frank suggested. "Let's see what happens." So the note lay on the table untouched for the next ten days. Frank occasionally surveyed his little congregation, which never numbered more than twenty-five, and wondered which one had written the note. He never found out.

In early August Frank led four baptismal candidates into the stormy breakers on the shore of the Caspian Sea. They, along with the Niewerts, formed the second church in Persia.

Three days later Frank headed for home, exchanging the tedious overland trip for a sea voyage to the port of Astara. When the regular large streamer from Baku failed to appear, he settled for passage on a small freight boat. Heavily loaded with bales of cotton, the boat had limited provisions for its thirty passengers, who had to spend the night sitting on the cotton bales on the deck.

At two a.m. when Frank had bedded himself down on a bale and fallen asleep, a violent storm suddenly swept over the ship. In moments the sea tossed itself up into mountains and then valleys of water, battering the ship, tearing at it, and rushing across the decks in violent swirls. The motor struggled in vain against the force of the wind. With every roll it seemed that the boat must capsize, but somehow it always righted itself. Together with the rising of the storm came the cries of the people—the screams of the women and the sobs of the children counterpointing the men's wails, "Allah the All Merciful, save us! Save us."

Frank considered his situation objectively. There seemed very little chance of reaching shore alive. "Oh God, whether I live or die—all is in Thy hands." If he should drown, then to disappear into the depths of the ocean until Jesus came was as good an end as any. On the other hand, his work in Persia seemed only now to have begun; and if he should live, he might yet see a great fulfillment of his lifelong dream. In that case there couldn't be enough water in the entire Caspian Sea to destroy him. Either way, he put himself at God's disposal. And since he had nothing further to worry about, he pulled his soggy blanket up over his head for protection from the rain and settled back down onto his cotton bale to sleep until sunrise.

After six hours at the mercy of the storm, the boat ended up at the point where it had started. Upon re-entering the harbor, passengers and crew alike rejoiced to set foot on solid earth again. The new believers welcomed Frank with tears and open arms. "We prayed for you the whole night. And God spared you for us."

A few hours of uncertain sunshine passed, and then the storm broke out again with new fury. Swollen rivers swept away houses and uprooted orchards. After three more days of the storm, a calm Sabbath dawned, and Frank spent another unscheduled day with the infant church. On Monday Brother Niewart returned unexpectedly from his assignment in Teheran in time to be ordained as the local church elder and have the little flock committed to his care.

Frank finally reached Astara safely by a large steamer and immediately took an overnight carriage to Ardebīl. Morning there brought scenes, the intensity of which he had never encountered before. This was the tenth day of Muharram, the Persian month of mourning.

As he passed through the streets, he met group after group of frenzied men and boys dressed in black and singing their lamentations for the martyrdom of Hussein, the grandson of the prophet Mohammed, which had happened in A.D. 680. But Frank turned his thoughts to home. In seven weeks he had traveled only 700 miles, but it seemed much more—both in time and distance.

And then he was with his family again—Florence in his arms

and the boys around his knees competing for attention. Everyone wanted to talk at once, and though news of his travels ranked high on the list of preferred subjects for conversation, the horrors of the ceremony of Muharram got equal time and more. Year after year the Oster boys were to sit on the wall of the mission compound, fascinated while they watched groups of people go by wielding their *ghamehs* (butcher knives).

"I guess at least eighteen died here in Tabriz today," Florence sighed. She was prone to faint at the sight of even a little blood. "I'm glad it's over for another year."

The Shi'a Moslems of Persia are probably more fanatical than the members of any other Moslem sect. Instead of making a pilgrimage to Mecca, as the Sunni Moslems do, they travel from Persia through Baghdad to Karbala and on to mystic Najaf in Mesopotamia. Near Najaf more human bodies lie buried together than in perhaps any other spot on earth. The corpses of the faithful who have been so unfortunte as to die far away from the sacred spot are "cured" (salted and dried) and brought by caravan to be buried in the holy ground around the city. In a sense, the dead might seem hopelessly lost in anonimity, but the Moslem believer will always assure an inquirer, "Allah knows all their names."

The boys would never forget the sight of those long files of "mourners" passing the place where they sat on the wall. The mourners came from the mosque, where they had spent the night listening to the tragic story of Hussein's defeat at Karbala, and pounding their heads at every mention of the martyr's name. Emotionally overwrought and wearing long black robes, they went through the city, each with his left hand thrown around the shoulder of the man to his left. At every step they simultaneously lifted their shining *ghamehs* and in one stroke of the right arm slashed their foreheads. Blood gushed into their eyes, onto their robes, and then drenched the streets. Anyone who died during this ceremony was guaranteed immediate entrance into heaven and was therefore not mourned.

Bystanders and foreigners who interferred in these moments of religious passion did so at their own peril. An army major, under appointment to be the American consul at Tabriz, unwisely chose the fanatical hours of the tenth of Muharram to photograph the ornamental brass water cistern in the public square. "He's poisoned our drinking water." A shriek went up from the celebrant. Instantly, a menacing crowd formed and stoned the man as he tried to get away in a passing carriage. He, however, kept on snapping pictures of the frenzied mob. He did reach the hospital safely, and the doctor started to treat his wounds in the operating room, however, the mob burst in through the doors and windows, hauled the man off the table and stabbed him to death. When the doctor finally got back to the body, he counted 125 dagger wounds, multiple skull fractures, a smashed jawbone, and broken ribs.

Frank and Florence always viewed the proceedings of the month of Muharram with a mixture of revulsion and admiration. "I always think," Frank remarked, "that we have much to learn from them in the matter of devotion and faith."

"Yes," Florence added. "And we can never hope to reach people like this with any less passion for Christ and His kingdom than they have for Allah and their hero saints. Nothing else will ever do."

A Turn of the Tide

The Osters' second term of service got off to an auspicious beginning in so many ways. Hard work—yes, endless days of it, from dawn until far into the night. But both Frank and Florence felt the high motivation that comes with seeing results. At *last* God's work had begun to prosper in Queen Esther's land, and that in itself was reward enough. It gave them strength to rise and meet the demands of every new day—demands which by ordinary human standards would be insurmountable.

Then Florence had to take a detour which lasted almost a year. For months she fought off her body's protests, working steadily at her many responsibilities; but in the end she had to give in and go to the American Presbyterian hospital. After surgery and nineteen days in the hospital, she came home to enforced rest and a recuperation which ultimately restored her to good health.

During her convalescence she had much time to think about what might be done concerning the perennial problem of the refugees. Continual handouts were neither financially possible for her and Frank, nor were they personally desirable for the recipients. If only she could provide some type of employment that would bring in funds from the outside.

Then she thought of one of the new members—a refugee from Turkey. Verjine Shirvanian knew how to make lovely Armenian needlework. Her plan blossomed out almost overnight, and soon twenty girls were meeting daily at the Oster home. Fascinated, Florence watched the yards of delicate lace, the dainty doilies, and the fancy handkerchiefs take shape under her eyes. Lo, a lace factory had been born right under her roof. She sent packages of the lace to her mother, now back home in Michigan from the South African term, and to her sister Vandella in Washington. Because these imports were the work of refugees and orphans trying to make a living, the lace could be brought in duty-free and sold.

The business expanded. The minute perfection of the stitchery was in itself a recommendation for sales. When Florence's mother displayed the luncheon sets and doilies at Battle Creek Sanitarium, she sometimes sold as much as $300 worth of lace in a single afternoon. The money, returned to Florence, then went back to the girls. At last they could experience the pleasure and pride of workmanship and the honor of wages earned.

Not a day passed without some demand for welfare work. "You know what Isaiah said about 'dealing bread to the hungry' and 'covering the naked'?" Florence said, looking up from her sewing machine as Frank came in late one evening. "I never dreamed I would have such a practical, front-line part in fulfilling that prophecy!"

"Yes, Floss," Frank studied the woolen fabric racing along under the presser foot. "I've often thought that what we have to do here is complete nonsense from the standpoint of economics. There's no rational way we could explain how we can make the money we get as salary each month go as far as it does."

"I've marveled at the same thing," Florence replied, as she snipped off the threads and turned the seam. "There's something of the miracle of the widow's meal and oil in it, I'm sure."

Esnet, the orphan from Urmia, still lived with them, along with Knarik, another orphan from Maragha. And now Satenik, a beautiful sixteen-year-old who had been thrown out of her home when she came to Frank's meetings, had recently moved in with them too.

Gegham Khanoyan, a devoted young Adventist from Bitlis, Turkey, first came on a general visit to the Osters. The visit was followed by other, more personal visits, until he and Satenik were married and went to Urmia to establish a Christian home there.

One family of twelve had enjoyed the congenial atmosphere about the place so much that they had stayed for six weeks. Visitors from everywhere constantly made the Oster home their own.

Work among the refugees, the Osters discovered, turned out to be a successful byproduct of Frank's evangelism in Tabriz. Many returned home to carry the gospel to villages where no worker had ever been before. The need for organized education, however, became increasingly essential. Frank had translated and added a number of Advent songs to the Presbyterian hymn book. Sabbath School lessons had been written out, mimeographed, and distributed. Permission to write or translate other literature, however, was virtually impossible to get. Obviously they had to plan for a school.

It began with Nanajan Badal of the Presbyterian mission in Urmia, who taught the Assyrians. Soon the school expanded to include another room for seventy-five Armenian children, who were taught by Baron Gagik, an experienced teacher and a new Adventist. Baron Gagik had been disinherited by his wealthy family when he became a Christian. In fact, for the past eight years his father had refused to speak to him. Florence taught English classes and studied Russian and Turkish at the same time. All in all, it made a full program—with the Bible, of course, as a core subject. The youngsters all sat on the floor to read and then stretched out on the floor full length to write. The ensuing rush to enroll children in the new school filled the two small rooms far beyond capacity.

And then came Dedo.

Dedo, determined to get a Christian education for her son Melcom, had taken the boy to the Catholic school in the Gala district of Tabriz. Then she went home to sit on the curb in front of her door. The warmth of the mid-December sun felt good on her rheumatic joints.

Presently an Assyrian neighbor came by. "Have you heard, Dedo, of that new school that's been opened?" She paused to let anticipation for the gossip she was about to pass on take strong root. "And such a foolish thing. They keep Saturday! They're Jews!"

"Well, being Jewish isn't so strange, is it?" Dedo wanted to know.

"No, but these people hold their meetings every night. And to prove that the Jews gained the victory over Christ, the rabbi's wife stands at the door at the close of the meeting with a pillow that represents Christ!" The talebearer glowed with enthusiasm over her task. "And do you know, she has a big pin that she gives to each one as they go out. And she asks them to pierce the pillow, as though they were piercing Christ in effigy!" Dedo stared wide-eyed, and the woman embellished her story with more comments—"Did you ever hear of such a thing? Such blasphemy! I saw it with my own—"

Just then Melcom rushed in. Dedo braced herself for yet another surprise. Here it wasn't even noon yet, and Melcom was home tugging at her skirts again and crying "Mamma! Mamma!"

"What on earth are you doing here, child?" Her attention shifted instantly from the neighbor's story to Melcom's plight.

"I don't know," he sobbed, "but the headmaster said he didn't have a place for me in his school." Melcom buried his head in Dedo's lap and wailed.

"But why? Why did he do that?" Dedo knew how Melcom had set his heart on learning.

"I dunno— He didn't explain. He just said there's no room."

Dedo jumped to her feet, rheumatism notwithstanding. Getting more precise directions as to the location of the curious Jewish school, she left her erstwhile informer with open mouth and swept off to the Adventist mission, Melcom in tow.

Florence listened carefully to Dedo's story and looked with compassion at the tear-stained face of the would-be scholar. What could be done? "I'm so sorry," she explained, "but there's absolutely no more room."

Dedo was never one to take a mere *No* as a final answer. "But, Mrs. Oster, my husband's been killed. It is very important now for me to make a good life for the boy," she pleaded. "He's a good, bright lad, you'll see. And he wants to learn so badly. Could you somehow—?"

Something within Florence urged her to make an exception— just one more. So a place was made in which to squeeze Melcom among the children already on the floor. Now Dedo Gasparian could go home well satisfied. Of course, she wasn't going to leave her son under the influence of such heretical teachings without making a thorough personal investigation. So that meant that she had to return for the meeting that evening to witness the "piercing ceremony." Moreover, the lovely young headmistress had invited her to come back. And that is what she intended to do.

She arrived early to inspect the pillow and pin in advance, if possible. Unfortunately the rabbi's wife wasn't there yet, so she took a seat near the door. She wanted an advantageous position for watching the piercing, and she cared little for Frank's preaching, short and warm as it was. Instead, she kept her eyes fixed on Florence, seated near the front. Sure enough, near the end of the meeting, she saw the rabbi's wife move quietly toward the rear of the room. And yes, just as her neighbor had said, the rabbi's wife carried a pillow.

The fires of rebellion and outrage flared up in Dedo's zealous Christian heart. She wanted to scream, but she managed to control herself. She waited until she saw the actual piercing!

Then Florence was seen biting a huge safety pin between her teeth—further confirmation of the rumor. Frank now came to his appeal, but Dedo was blind and deaf to all as Florence began the piercing ceremony. But what was that? A little squeal, almost a chirp, from the pillow! Then Dedo smiled. So! *That* was it! *Khanoom* Oster was just changing her baby's diaper.

Dedo sighed and relaxed for the first time in two hours. She even tried to join in singing part of the closing hymn. Yes, Melcom would be permitted to continue in the Adventist School. And how silly her neighbor would feel when Dedo got through with her!

Melcom Gasparian proved to be all that his mother claimed him to be. After elementary school, he attended the local Armenian high school, faithfully keeping Sabbath all the way, until finally he graduated with honors and a two-year scholarship. He is now an ordained minister in Iran, and an effective worker.

Time went on, and ultimately, of course, something had to be done about the crowded condition of the school. "It's the irresistible force and immovable object, Frank," Florence complained. "It's impossible to walk across the room without stepping on children."

Then, just when the frustration seemed unbearable, a large building near the mission compound came up for rent. Usta Ovdishoo, a very good Seventh-day Adventist carpenter, made benches and tables so the children would be off the mud floor. The crowds, of course, didn't diminish. With the new building came the possibility of having more teachers, and the enrollment shot up to 300.

Under Florence's supervision other schools soon opened in Salma, Urmia, and Maragha, bringing the total number of students to about 500. Ultimately the growing influence of these schools came to the attention of local religious leaders, and one day Florence received a call to visit the head man of the Armenian Church.

"What do you think he wants, Frank?" Florence asked, an uneasiness akin to fear gnawing at her.

"I don't know, Floss." Frank drew her close. "But I'll be praying for you all through the interview. And I'm very certain that you'll know exactly the right things to say."

The head man asked many probing questions. Florence assured him that the Adventist schools carried out the full academic program of the state. The children, she pointed out, were also learning Farsi (the national language) as well as English and the language of their parents too. Moreover, all the teachers were fully qualified.

"But why do you refuse to have school on Saturdays, as is the custom here?" the head man wanted to know. Here was Florence's chance for a quick explanation of the Ten Commandments and the place of the fourth within them. "Well," the man mused, "go ahead and do it that way. It's all right, if you can keep up with the curriculum, as you seem to be doing."

As Florence rose to leave, the head man stopped her. "One more question," he said. "I want to know why these young people who have been baptized as babies in the Armenian Church must be dipped in again. Isn't one baptism good enough?"

Now Florence knew she had to say just the right thing here, and she prayed immediately for the correct words. "When Jesus was baptized," she said, "He *went down into* the water and then *came up out* of it. We must do it *His* way, you see?"

The man shook his head in puzzlement. "Go ahead and do that too, if you must." He smiled down on her benevolently as he showed her to the door.

To balance off her many public responsibilities, Florence always had an ample share of crises on the domestic front. At one point, the three Oster boys contracted trachoma—a disease which, if not cured, could hinder their re-entry into the United States. The local remedy, however, was violent. The doctor gave them a small stone called a hell-stone. Their inner eyelids had to be rubbed with this hell-stone both morning and evening. Florence cringed with pain herself at every treatment, for the stone burned the boys frightfully and sent them to bed crying every night. Heartbreaking a task as it was, Florence persevered, and the boys' eyes healed, remarkably enough.

Another painful disease, which became Winton's exclusive trial, was *kachal*—a scalp sore which refused to heal. He picked it up on a boat-crossing of Lake Urmia while accompanying Frank on one of his itineraries. The Turkish soldiers had fun talking to him in Turkish and pretending that he too was a soldier. They took turns putting their caps on the lad's head and saluting. From the passing of the caps he contracted *kachal*.

When several doctors had failed to effect a cure, Sister Javaher, the Jewish widow, made a hopeful offer. "You give Winton to me, and I'll guarantee that he gets over the *kachal*."

Sister Javaher took Winton home and plastered his head with a gum from a tree, which the Persians chewed like chewing gum. "She says I've got to keep it on for a whole month," Winton announced upon his return. Although he wasn't old enough at the time to be concerned about the appearance of his thick gum skullcap, the affair was still depressing.

"Well, nothing else has worked," Florence comforted. "So I guess we'll have to try it her way." She had no option but to give Winton up to the dictates of folk medicine.

At the end of the month Winton returned to his benefactor. Javaher sat him down on a stool and said, "Hold on tight while I pull the *sagez* off. It's going to hurt." "Hurt" turned out to be a massive understatement, and after violent tugging and twisting, all the hair that had grown up into the *sagez* came off as the helmet finally was wrenched loose.

Poor Winton ran a high fever as a result of his suffering, but by the time he had recovered from that—behold, the *kachal* was gone! His hair grew back, and he was thus spared having to spend the rest of his life with big scar patches where no hair could grow.

In the next year, 1925, another important event in the saga of missions in Persia occurred. Of course, it had a far-reaching effect on the Osters' personal lives too. For fourteen years Frank and Florence had never had a visitor from outside the country to call on them. Mails had sometimes been detained for as long as twelve months at a stretch. Money transfers, frequently delayed, demanded ingenuity, resourcefulness, and extreme economy. Travel was incredibly slow.

For years the Osters had been writing to the European Division for help. They received letters full of encouragement and kind thoughts, but no real commitments. Consequently when they received word that Dr. Henry Hargreaves, a young English doctor, would join them in their missionary endeavors, they felt a wholly new kind of exuberance and zest for their work. Just before his arrival they were able to rent a lovely compound to house the growing school, the mission offices, the Oster residence, and a meticulously manicured garden. And in honor of the new scope of their outreach, they set aside a large room for the doctor to set up a medical office.

The arrival of the eagerly anticipated doctor in Tabriz coincided closely with yet another celebration of the tenth of Muharram. The city fathers requested the new physician to come to the mosque to treat the victims.

"Why don't I treat them at the hospital?" Hargreaves wanted to know. "*Must* they be treated in the mosque?"

"Yes, they must, Henry—by all means," Frank said. "Their wounds are of religious origin, and therefore, the treatment must partake of the same elements."

Often a *ghameh*-wielder, filled with more zeal than skill, would bring the knife down more vigorously than he intended and split his skull open. As many as a hundred such casualties in Tabriz yearly was no novelty. The man who acted the part of the villain, Shimr, was often set upon and beaten unmercifully. Sometimes he died.

In the battle of Karbala it was Shimr who had, with his cavalry, closed in on Hussein and wounded him mortally with an arrow. Then, in a calculated burst of savagery, the horsemen had trampled Hussein's heroic band into the earth. The victors carried seventy heads back to Kufa (Al Kufah). There Shimr had scornfully turned the head of Hussein over with his staff, like a loathsome fruit fallen off a tree. An aged Arab among the bystanders had murmured, "Gently, gently. It is the grandson of the prophet. By Allah. I've seen these very lips kissed by the blessed mouth of

Mohammed. See *A History of Persia* by Sykes, vol. 1, p. 541.

The passions of civil strife had not abated, not even in 1200 years. So the figure of the despised Shimr aroused almost more hatred now than had Shimr himself back on the battlefield of Karbala. "If you have this year's Shimr among your patients today, Henry, you'll have a major repair job on your hands, I daresay," Frank advised the doctor, as Henry headed out to hail a carriage to take him to the mosque. Winton, who had quickly come to admire Dr. Hargreaves, accompanied him.

The relationship between the twenty-five-year-old doctor and the eight-year-old boy had double benefits. Winton acted as his interpreter when he made sick calls, and proved to be an efficient little helper at a time when few persons could translate Turkish into English. And he needed no urging to hang around and help Dr. Hargreaves when he was treating patients at the office either.

At home Winton now zealously practiced medicine on his younger brothers, in imitation of the wonderful Dr. Hargreaves. He would tap their chests, have them stick out their tongues and say "Ah", feel their pulses, and inquire after their health until the little fellows begged to be allowed to get up off the floor and play at being well. The seeds of ambition sown in Winton's heart in those days, however, blossomed into full fruition many years later when Winton himself became a doctor and could tap chests and ask questions to his heart's content.

One day the gatekeeper opened the door of the compound in response to a stormy barrage of knocking. To the intense alarm of all within, a number of Kurdish men on horseback stood outside. The gateman fled to Frank's office. "Oh, Oster Agha. . . . Oh, Agha. The Kurds! A band of Kurds stands at our gate." The man trembled, seized with a sudden palsy.

Frank went to the gate. "*Khoda bashad posht o panah shoma* [God be with you. What is your wish?]"

"We understand that you have an eye doctor here," they replied. "We urgently need his services for our chief, Simco."

"Ah, Agha," murmured the gateman, behind Frank's back. "Simco is the very one who has been conducting the latest Kurdish raids. He knows nothing but to kill."

The men waited with ill-disguised impatience. "The chief has injured his eye," they went on, fingering their daggers meaningfully. "You must send your doctor to heal him. And he must come with us now."

A hasty consultation with the doctor followed, along with a fervent time of prayer. Frank agreed that Henry should go. To refuse such an invitation could mean disaster for the mission. "I don't doubt that the call is genuine," Henry said. "I don't believe it's a trap."

Frank saw yet another possibility. "Accepting this call, Henry, could open up a whole new direction for our work. Do you realize that this is the first time we've had a request from Moslems, even if they are Kurds?"

"Right, Frank! Working for the Christian minorities here has been hard enough, I know." Henry had started laying out instruments and medicines to fill his bag. "But I do keep thinking of that vast Moslem world out there, still untouched. And who knows? Perhaps I'm on my way now." He grinned as he snapped his bag shut.

The mission family came together for earnest prayer and all felt both sadness and uncertainty as their doctor rode away on the spare horse that the Kurds had brought for him. "Daddy, Dr. Hargreaves won't have me to help him this time." Winton sounded both wistful and worried.

"No, Son," Frank said, looking down at the boy as he turned to go back to his office. "On this call, he'll need help far beyond anything any of us could give. Remember to pray for him especially, while he's gone on this trip. He needs it."

"Oh, yes, I surely will." Winton peered down the street at the rapidly disappeaing band of horsemen.

"And, by the way, how would you like to go with me on my next trip to Urmia and Salmas? I could use some help too, you know."

"Oh, Daddy! Can I?" Winton did a little hop and jump back through the gateway. "When will we start?"

Dr. Hargreaves, meanwhile, found that the Kurdish chief did indeed have a very bad eye. He immediately began treatment with ointments and hot-and-cold packs. As the days went by, the eye improved steadily. He dared not think what the results might have been had the matter gone otherwise! Hospitably entertained in the Kurdish camp, he could complain of nothing, except that after a week he felt an urgency about getting back to Tabriz and his many patients there whom he had deserted so unceremoniously.

After the treatment one morning, he paused before bowing himself out of the great man's presence. "These men of yours have watched me care for your eye. They can easily continue the treatments that I have been giving you, and I'm sure that in a very short time your eye will be perfectly well." Now he had to come to the point. "I—ah—I have patients down in the valley who are all waiting for me. I must return to them now."

"No! Absolutely not! the chief thundered. "We will not let you go until my eye is completely healed!"

Stunned, Hargreaves began again, "But there are many people, you see. Surely, if—" But Simco neither looked nor listened, and the doctor knew that his pleas fell on deaf ears.

Yet, not wholly deaf, however, for after considerable remonstrance Simco blew a whistle; and the doctor was instantly surrounded by a cordon of Kurdish warriors, armed to the teeth. He needed no one to explain to him that if he pressed his point any further, he would never escape with his life.

So, trusting God to care for his patients in Tabriz, he stayed with the mountain chief until the eye was completely healed. On several occasions the doctor improved the time by speaking to Simco of Jesus and His love. Amid all his insecurity he claimed a particular promise that had special meaning for him there, "Trust in the Lord and do good, and He shall bring it to pass." And that gave him faith to believe that ultimately he *would* reach home in safety.

The church, meanwhile, prayed for him continually and rejoiced in his return when a band of Kurds delivered him at the same gate from which they had forcibly taken him away two weeks earlier. On departure the outlaws presented him with the fine horse on which he had ridden down from the mountain—a gift of the chief.

A few days later another band of Kurds delivered a cow at the gate, "for the skilled doctor." And about a week after that a sheep was sent down for him. "Payment on the installment plan," Henry remarked.

"Yes," Frank added, "and gift-giving in the best Moslem tradition. By sending the presents down at intervals they are demonstrating to us not only the chief's personal thanks but also his *continued* appreciation for your services."

His first experience among the Kurds impressed Dr. Hargreaves for the rest of his life with the needs of the untouched millions of Moslems. He longed for the day when a concerted effort to solve this problem would be made. After years of service in Persia he made an appeal to the Sabbath Schools on this point in the *Sabbath School Mission Quarterly:* "Our medical work has brought us into daily contact with Moslems.... It seems to us that, properly supported and organized for evangelism, the medical work can be a potent factor in carrying the last warning message to these people."

The doctor soon won his way into the hearts of the people. As Henry learned the language, Winton continued to accompany him just for the thrill of the job. The mission work was now on a firm footing, and the doctor skillfully shared the burdens of administration. The mission property, with the adjoining school, had been purchased; and the first church building had been erected on a broad avenue in another part of Tabriz. Several new national workers joined the mission force, including Brother Vagharshak Shirvanian. He had killed many people in his flight from Turkey, but now he laid aside his weapons to take up the sword of the Spirit and help many to live. His zeal matched that of his wife, who worked tirelessly among the girls in the lace factory.

The year 1926 brought another bonus to the mission work when Dr. Arsen Arzoo came home to Persia with a newly conferred degree from Loma Linda's College of Medical Evangelists. He set up practice in his hometown of Isfahan, thus augmenting the efforts of the infant church there. In the same year the Oscar Olson family arrived from Sweden to open the training school and relieve Florence of some of her school administration tasks.

Along with the Olsons came another blessing in the form of Elder W. E. Read, the European Division Secretary of Foreign Missions. He spent two months in Persia traveling, counseling, encouraging, and being astonished. Perhaps nothing intrigued him more than the roads.

"I see a surprising number of automobiles here, Brother Oster," he remarked.

"Oh, yes. Persia's working itself into the twentieth century with much determination these days," Frank affirmed. "We've seen enormous changes in our time here."

"But the roads! Really!" Elder Read couldn't find the next word.

"Yes, they *are* pretty bad—hardly deserving of the name, I guess," Frank admitted.

The visitor smiled. "Why not just call them 'ways'? When I see the cars just go bounding out over the open countryside, it seems the proper word should just refer to a general direction and not too any material route for getting there."

"True," Frank replied. "You can't depend on the evidence of your eyes, for you can seldom tell a road from the desert for miles around. Still, the chauffeurs always seem to know."

One day in early 1927 Frank walked in with a letter. "Surprise, Floss. The General Conference is inviting us to take another furlough."

"Furlough? How marvelous!" Florence's mind leaped instantly to a thousand joyful possibilities. Home! Mother, Father, sisters, friends—a total new education for the boys. The ideas tumbled over in her mind in reckless confusion. Then she remembered. "And hasn't God arranged it well?"

"Most certainly." Frank agreed. "Henry's here to take the administrative responsibilities, and we have a substantial mission staff to keep things going." Frank sat down and spread the letter out on the table before them. "No sickness, no war! Wonderful!"

"We've got every reason to make it a true vacation," Florence said, as she drummed her fingers on the table and looked out the window and across the garden. "You know Frank, our work here seems to have reached a certain 'ripeness' that makes it easy to think of taking a little rest just now. It's hard to explain."

"I know what you mean, Floss. It's rather like taking a series of hard examinations and then suddenly walking into a kind of graduation that you hadn't had time to think about very much. And yet you know that it's right, and that this is the time to go."

Florence laughed. "Let's go and hunt up those old packing boxes. We haven't thought about them for *five years*. And, as for hard examinations, we'll be back here in our 'character training school' again before we know it."

Celebrations of the New Look

The Osters' second furlough proved to be routine in many ways, as compared with their first departure from Persia. By car to Baghdad, in convoy across the Syrian Desert to Lebanon, and then the voyage across the Mediterranean and Atlantic to New York—the whole excursion passed without trauma.

The Washington stop called for medical repairs—dental work, tonsillectomies for the boys, and such. Vacation with Father and Mother White in Charlotte, Michigan came next, and by September everyone was ready for the opening of school at Emmanuel Missionary College (now Andrews University).

For the boys it meant their first time in school with teachers other than their mother. Florence herself reveled in being a student again. The many years of initiating, organizing, pouring out, and giving of herself made the stimulation of being a student in a college classroom again more precious to her than ever before. As for Frank, he worked steadily all through that Michigan winter not only visiting churches and pastoring but also translating tracts—vital messages which a fearful but seeking Moslem might read in his home before he had mustered enough courage to attend a public Christian meeting. Then, the final quick trip to visit relatives in the western states pronounced the benediction upon Frank and Florence's second furlough.

Friends sent them back with a phonograph and a collection of records, along with other things common enough at home but unique on the other side of the world. And Florence's energetic friend, Mrs. Alma Wiles, (an Australian nurse with a mission story all of her own) raised $300 for Osters to get a well for a clean water supply. The stories of the water in the cisterns had shocked her into service and productive concern.

Times were changing in other ways too. Now Frank and Florence took a Chevrolet back to the mission field. The convenience brought about by this substitute for donkeys, horses, wagons, camels, and carriages quite staggered the imagination. Indeed, the car promised to open up all kinds of new possibilities in their Persian life. "And what a clever idea that American Automobile Association Trip-Tic is." From an upper deck of their ship at the New York dock, Florence looked down on the freight-loading activities.

"And there she goes!" said Frank. They both watched their car swing wide, as the crane hoisted it into the ship's hold.

"If the Trip-Tic works as promised," Florence said, "that means that we should be able to drive all the way across Europe without unloading our car for customs at every border, doesn't it?"

"And what a blessing *that* will be," Frank sighed. "I keep trying not to remember how many times we loaded and unloaded on our last trip into Persia. Twenty-three, didn't you say?"

The journey across Europe turned out to be everything that could be hoped for. The scenery proved to be all that had ever been promised for loveliness. Then the opportunity to attend the Central European Union Conference meetings in Darmstadt, Germany, added real spiritual refreshment to the material pleasures they had already enjoyed.

The Sunday they drove through Bulgaria, however, provided the adventure and tension which had hitherto been lacking. The potholes in the narrow roads; the endless streams of wagons, oxcarts, and cars; and the throngs of pedestrians made the passage down into Turkey a stressful but memorable one.

"Hey, Dad!" Winton shouted. "Look! Our bedroll is gone off the back of the car!" The relaxed holiday mood which had prevailed for most of the journey faded away like a whiff of smoke.

Frank eased the car off onto the rock shoulder of the road, and all four doors burst open simultaneously. It was too true. The whole family stood and looked at the frayed ends of rope hanging impotently from the bumper.

"Oh, dear! How *could* it be!" Florence felt like sitting down on the bank and wailing like a funeral mourner. Did they have to lose something *every* time they came to Persia?

Frank fingered a rope end. "Imagine that! The bumps wore these ropes right through."

"I guess that last big hole must have snapped it right off, huh?" Francis stood by his father, foot on the bumper in a man-to-man stance.

"But Frank! Those blankets—and the clothes! We can't replace them anywhere outside of the States." Tears welled up in Florence's eyes, and she didn't try to fight them down. It all seemed too much, altogether too much.

"Well, of course, we have only one thing left to do, Floss. The usual—" Frank replied. So they all stood around the back of the car while Frank prayed that the precious bundle would be recovered.

Florence's courage and perhaps her faith too, were still diminished. They didn't know the language, so how could they ask any questions? And what peasant could resist the temptation to keep such an obviously valuable roll of bedding? Frank turned the car around, and they slowly retraced their journey. The futility of it all pierced Florence like a dagger stab.

Then it was seven-year-old Kenneth's turn to shout, "Daddy! Daddy! See that man in the wagon there? He's waving at us."

Sure enough, from a cart on the opposite side of the road, a man called to them in broken German, *"Halt! Halt! I' werd' Ihnen glei' was erzähl'n* [Stop! I will tell you something]!"

The man knew a language they would understand! Had the miracle begun already? Frank barely got the car stopped before the voluble peasant was at the window, dramatizing his story. Six miles back he had seen the bundle fall off the car and had picked it up and taken it to the police station. *"Entschuldigung* [I'm so sorry]!" he said repeatedly. "I didn't know I would see you again. Forgive."

"Don't apologize, my friend," Frank exclaimed. "You've helped us very much, and we are very thankful."

"Here is my son. Allow him to go back with you and show you the way." The man beckoned the alert, black-eyed youth holding the horses. "Come, go with the strangers to help them."

A short time later, with the bedding roll safely tied onto the back of the car again with new rope, Florence felt that she could hug and kiss everybody! How could she have thought that God would lose sight of their bundle for even a moment. "Let's sing the doxology," she cried. And they did. Then the boys wanted to sing their Sabbath School "thank-You song" too. So, amid song and rejoicing, the Chevrolet jounced on down the road toward Istanbul.

At the Turkish border Frank had to hand over $100 for "honor money." Florence was exasperated. "But the Trip-Tic *guarantees* that we won't sell the car in Turkey."

"They promise us a refund when we leave the country, Floss," Frank pulled out his wallet with a sigh. "Trip-Tic means nothing to them. They're their own people—you know that."

The stopover in Istanbul allowed time for doing the family laundry and letting tired, road-weary bodies rest and limber up for the last stage of their journey. Fewer bumps but more dust marked Turkish highways, until the guard at a checkpoint called them to a sudden halt well within Turkey's eastern borders. "Why are we stopped here," Florence wanted to know, when Frank emerged from the police outpost.

"There's a military zone ahead, and we aren't allowed to drive through it. We'll have to take the train."

"The train?" Whatever's going to happen to the car and all the things we have in it?" Florence had nightmare visions of receiving the mere shell of a Chevrolet when it got to the border.

"They promise to put the car on the train with us."

"I wonder!" Later, as they went to board the train, Florence cast anxious backward glances at the beloved Chevrolet.

"Come, Floss. Don't be like Lot's wife." Frank hurried the family into the railroad car, where the curtains were tightly drawn across the windows. They had been forbidden to look out upon the military secrets of Turkey.

"But *why* can't we look out the windows," Kenneth wanted to know.

"It's so dark in here," Winton grumbled.

"And so boring too," Francis added, as he slumped down into his seat and scowled.

"All right, boys," Florence announced in her best classroom voice. "Since we can't see what's going on outside, this would be a good time to play a guessing game, don't you think?"

Hours later when they arrived at the border, Florence's worst premonitions were realized. The car was *not* on the train. The officers told them they had decided that a driver should bring the car down.

"But why didn't you tell us this before?" Even Frank seemed to be nearing the thin edge of his patience.

The man shrugged. "It was not convenient, Agah."

"Indeed, it's not convenient!" Frank exclaimed. "How shall we get a driver now?"

"You must hire one. We will arrange it."

"But a driver we've never even seen?" Florence didn't approve of this kind of guessing game at all.

"We've no choice," Frank said. "Go ahead."

The car arrived in good condition, surprisingly enough, and Florence realized that she had let her emotions boil high for no purpose. God, as usual, had their affairs in hand, regardless of what the surface events might portend.

One more frustration awaited them at the border, however, when they went to reclaim their $100. They had to wait a day while the immigration officers rounded up the honor money. "Just wait. We have to go only to the next town to get it."

Upon their return Frank offered them a tip for honesty—if not efficiency—but they refused. "It is not necessary," they declared with pride. "Only report of us that the Turkish government honored its promise."

The uncertain strip of dirt road that remained straggled through Syria and Iraq and on into Persia. It produced it's own share of tire trouble, carburetor trouble, and almost every other kind of trouble a car can suffer in traveling many days on bumpy, dusty roads.

At home again in Tabriz, they unloaded the Chevrolet. It stood like a tired horse before the gate, its glossy black hide enveloped in layers of dust. "And it was a *new* car when we left Michigan," Florence marveled. "Poor thing!"

"It has served well, Floss," Frank reminded her, as he reached for the last boxes hidden under the back seat. "And, as the Bible says, it's good to learn to 'bear the yoke in . . . youth.' I suspect the car is going to have an eventful career here. Its already extensive experience has matured it a good deal, no doubt."

Their freight arrived in mid-December, five months after being shipped from the States. "Floss," Frank said, "I want to get on with building the garage for the car. Why don't you take Haik and go clear our goods through customs. Haik can take off some time from the garden work."

That seemed fair enough. After all, the faithful Chev deserved the reward of shelter and comfort. All the same Florence wished she had Frank's know-how. He had been through the ordeal so many times. As she watched the officials go through the shipment item by item, recording in detail the contents of each box, she could only pray that the duty would be reasonable. No visible policies governed duties—they seemed to be determined by the whim of the moment.

Finally the officers reached the last box. "It is now late, Khanoom Oster. We are very tired." Certainly no one could deny the zeal with which they had pursued their task. "We won't go through the last box tonight. Tomorrow we will finish."

Florence had no choice but to leave. Should she press the matter, she might materially worsen the situation. "There was nothing else I could do," she told Frank that night.

"Yes, Floss. I guess that's all you could do." Frank frowned. "But I still don't like the looks of things."

Early the next morning Florence and Haik returned to the customhouse. "Well, we found nothing of special value in your belongings," the customs official remarked. "So we decided not to bother opening the last box. Just take your things home."

Florence felt like singing, dancing, and shouting the praises of the benevolent official behind the desk. Frank's uneasiness had turned out to be unfounded after all. She hailed the first *doroshkeh* (carriage) she found and hired a wagon to carry the things home.

In triumph she burst into Frank's partially closed-in garage. "Oh Frank, we didn't have to pay any duty—not even one penny. Can you believe it?"

Frank stood up. "None at all? That's very unusual, but certainly very fortunate." He dusted the sawdust off his overalls. "Let's go then and look at our treasures. It's been a long time since we saw them.

Recovering so many personal belongings at once caused excitement to run high all around. "Looks as if we don't need to plan for any Christmas presents next week," Frank speculated. "You're all getting the same effect just from seeing all the old stuff."

"Oh, yes, Daddy, let's have Christmas." Kenneth looked anxious, as he pulled his favorite old teddy bear from a trunk, and hugged him tight. "I haven't seen my bear for *so long.*"

Joy died quickly, however, after the trunks had been emptied and the opening of the boxes began. Obviously, strange hands had meddled with every one of them. Out of four dozen jars of fruit (all of which had been painstakingly packed), one dozen were broken. In another food box cocoa, baking powder, breakfast cereal, and beans had been mixed together as if for some grotesque new recipe.

But the worst was yet to come. Francis opened his violin case to find the violin gone. He wept and couldn't be comforted. "Oh, Frank, your new Prince Albert suit and your spring overcoat are gone." Florence pawed through the last box which had not been opened at the customhouse—at least not when she had been there. "The lovely rose bedspread Aunt Ella made for us! Oh, dear, it's gone." She sat down to mingle her tears with those of Francis. "Why did I ever leave the boxes unattended, even for a moment."

The final blow came minutes later when Frank came and gently put his arms around her. "I'm so sorry, my darling, but the phonograph is gone too."

Florence felt almost the last heartstring snap. "The phonograph! Oh, no, Frank. Not that too?" The tears rushed on anew. "The canned stuff is all right, but my precious canned music? How shall we live without it?"

"But I insured everything before we left New York, Floss. Remember? We'll get some money back."

Florence looked through teary eyes at the weeping children, each with his own personal little tragedy too. Feeling very small and forsaken, she took off her glasses and buried her face on Frank's shoulder again. "But I don't want the money. I just want music."

"There, there, dear one. Cry then awhile," Frank patted her head. "We'll feel better after a while, and then, of course, we'll go on."

And, of course, they did go on. By 1929 their long, lonely pioneer struggle had become a thing of the past. The very memory of hardships became buried under the excitement of the growing mission work. For Frank there was the increased church membership—up to 140 now. Then there was that new interest over in

Hamadan, the ancient home of Esther and Mordecai, with its colony of 200 Jews inquiring after the Christians who kept Sabbath and abstained from eating swine's flesh.

Florence now had more time for helping the boys with their school lessons. Her chores as secretary-treasurer of the mission had been lightened when Elder Read had shown her a new system of bookkeeping which made accurate accounting much less time-consuming.

In the field, six evangelists preached in Armenian, Assyrian, and Russian to the minority groups of central and northwest Persia. In 1928 the Arzoos and the Olsons joined forces in the city of Sultanabad (now Arak), opening simultaneously a clinic and a school for Moslems. The doctor sent an urgent call for a lady physician to come and serve the still tradition-bound women of the land. Then the teacher complained of a lack of space, when the enrollment quadrupled itself in less than two years.

In 1930 the church headquarters transferred to the capital, Tehran, and the field divided into two missions, with the West Persia Mission coming under the supervision of Pastor Tulaszewski from Germany.

While the mission work made dramatic progress, the very fabric of the culture of Persia slowly changed around them. The land began to emerge from the slumber of the ages. His Majesty Reza Shah Pahlavi launched the nation into a series of reforms, the results of which could scarcely be imagined at the start.

First, a census needed to be taken so that military training could be enforced. Without any family names, however, the people could not be organized for registration. Hence, the directive that everyone must identify himself, not merely as "Ali, the son of Hasan" or "Parviz, the son of Iraj," but by a distinguishing family name. In the ensuing scramble to secure names, opportunists cashed in on the emergency. Creative entrepreneurs sitting outside the city hall made up hitherto unknown names and sold them for as much as $500 apiece. Dissension divided families. The teacher, Miss Nanjan Badal, couldn't agree with her two brothers on the selection of a common name, so each appropriated one of his own making. The faithful Haik, lately promoted to the position of gatekeeper, took the name "Adventist" as his surname as well as spiritual name. Hence all his family, whatever their religious preference, would be known as "Adventist."

More problems arose over ages. No one knew for sure how old he was, so the field was open for adjustments of all kinds. People usually dated themselves in relation to some important event—often a Kurdish raid. Because of frequency, this notion only added to the confusion. Older people took the chance to become younger, and the younger hoping to sidestep military service added a decade or two to their approximate age. Marvelous relationships resulted, as in the case of the man who gave his age as being two years younger than that of his son, who, at the same time, tried to evade being drafted into the army.

In the end, everyone settled on a new name and a birthday, and this information was recorded on his new identity card. At this point, freedom of choice ended. The appalling severity of military discipline broke the spirits of all but the stoutest. One soldier who tried to run away was beaten with 200 stripes on his bare back, while one officer sat on his head and another on his feet. If he cried out, the number automatically doubled. He fainted and was carried to the hospital, only to be dragged out six days later to be whipped again. So, at this awful pace, Persia prepared for war in the best way she knew.

A heavy cloak of superstition still enveloped the minds of the people, woven from thousands of years of legend and folklore. Mere twentieth-century technology could not dislodge it—no, not even with the proofs spread out for all to see. Esnat, the Osters' long-time maid, knew very well that the earth couldn't rotate around the sun. "I myself saw the sun go down and drop into a big well when I lived in Shiraz," she declared.

At the Persian New Year at the time of the vernal equinox, one visitor regarded Frank and Florence with fine scorn because they didn't feel the earth move at eleven o'clock that morning when the transition of seasons occurred. "Of course, the earth rests on the point of a great cow's horn, and when the cow is tired on New Year's Day, she shifts the earth to the other horn. You must have felt it," the man said. "And the cow, as we all know, stands on the back of a great fish."

Then there was the man at the evangelistic meeting who took exception to the increase of earthquakes being cited as a sign of the end. "No, of course, not!" he objected. "There is a very obvious reason for earthquakes. Men are building such high buildings and piling so much weight on the earth, no wonder it shakes beneath them."

"But, friend, the buildings here are no more than three stories high," Frank countered.

"No matter. It's too heavy. Man is causing his own earthquakes." You can't beat that kind of logic, and Frank didn't try.

Florence's mind wandered back to the concrete "gorges" among New York City's skyscrapers. "What *would* the poor man say of them? He would accept them as a sign of something, to be sure! And he'd be right on that point, at least."

The shah hastened modernization on at a great pace. He realized that fanatical religious ideas had retarded the country's progress also, and he struck at the roots of many traditional practices. The head-cutting parades of the tenth Muharram were outlawed. And then came the question of prayers. The good Moslem always went through a series of genuflections as he knelt, bringing his forehead down to the prayer stone, as he faced in the direction of Mecca.

However with the introduction of the *Kolah Pahlavi* a certain type of hat, complications arose. The shah designed the hat to be worn in his honor and modeled it after the French military hat, with a little sunshade over the eyes, a flat top, and stiff sides. With the brim in front, of course, it was impossible to pray with the forehead to the ground. To pray with uncovered head would be unthinkable. So the worshiper turned the hat around with the visor at the back—which was practical, except for the forgetful elderly people who didn't remember to reverse the hat and then got arrested for dishonoring the shah by wearing the Pahlavi hat backwards.

Then overnight the Pahlavi hat was outlawed. Men were required to wear the conventional European felt hat with the brim all around. The young people gradually were weaned from the conservative forms of prayer while the oldsters faithfully carried around special prayer hats for the appropriate times.

If the men's problems were disturbing, those of the women were horrendous. The shah recognized the necessity of liberating the women of Persia from the chador (veil) and thereby reordering their whole position in the country. Another royal decree went forth. By a certain date—after a forty-day incubation period for the idea—no veiled women should appear on the streets. No faithful Moslem woman would ever permit her face to be seen in public, and the seriousness of this move shook Persia to its foundations. Still, no one wanted to prevent the breath-taking progress of His Majesty's program of modernization. It had an attractive, exhilarating momentum all its own; and somehow the transition was achieved with only minimal bloodshed.

On the first day of the decree, Frank came home with a quizzical smile on his face. Florence could remember every moment of her dreadful encounter many years before when she'd gone to the Maragha bazaar unveiled. "How is it going, Frank? Are the women *really* on the streets unveiled?"

"Well, if they aren't, they'll soon become so," he replied.

"What do you mean?"

"Why, there are policemen on every corner tearing the veils off the women," Frank laughed. "It would be funny, if it weren't so pathetic. Stacks of chadors are piled on the street corners."

Florence thought of all those poor women who, in the traditions of the centuries, had lived in demur privacy behind those veils. "I feel so sorry for them. It must be like walking naked in public. What a terrible ordeal!"

"Yes, Floss, I'm sure it is, but some of them are pretty resourceful." Frank started laughing again and sat down in the rocking chair to enjoy it more thoroughly. "You'd never guess what I saw just a couple of blocks from here, over on Naderi Avenue."

Florence sat down too to enjoy the moment with Frank. His heavy responsibilities seldom left him much leisure to enjoy the humor of the passing scene. "What happened?"

"An officer snatched the veil from an elderly woman," Frank went on. "In the shock, she sort of froze, at first. Then she squatted down, picked up all her skirts and pulled them over her head, and just walked off."

Florence laughed now. "Well! So nobody was going to force her to uncover her face. Good for her! Of course, I am in sympathy with what the shah is trying to do for the country." Florence paused. "And then what did the officer do?" she finally asked.

"What *could* he do," Frank shrugged. "He dropped the veil on the pile and just watched her go. I don't believe the shah has issued any decree yet to deal with a case like hers, though he may have to do so before he's finished, I'd venture to say."

Florence, of course, understood better than Frank the psychological battles taking place in the women's minds. To have a man other than her own husband see her face was a woman's supreme embarrassment. In comparison to that, walking down the street with her *gir-shalvar* (bloomers) showing was a less unacceptable alternative.

Days went on, and the papers were full of the backwash of the forced unveiling of the women. One army officer purchased European clothes for his wife and daughter in accordance with the royal decree. When they had put the garments on and presented themselves to him, he was so appalled by the prospect of his womenfolk being so disgraced in public that something within him just snapped loose. He pulled out his gun and shot the two women, and then turned it on himself. Death with honor rather than life with disgrace.

Yes, the emergence of Persia into the twentieth century came with grief and bloodshed. "But when the upheaval and the pain of it has passed," Frank mused one evening several weeks later, "the progress of Christianity in this country will show notable changes, I'm sure."

"It used to be that you could recognize a Moslem by his dress, but now—" Florence couldn't help wondering about the wisdom and feasibility of such rapidly enforced changes. "I wonder, sometimes, if it has been too much, too soon."

"You're right, Floss," Frank replied. "It would almost seem so. And yet, coming as it has, hand in hand with the new successes in our mission work, I believe the Lord can use these hard-come-by reforms to prepare Persia for hearing her last-day invitation into Christ's kingdom."

A Swiss Detour

The urgency and progress of the work brought no relaxation. Instead, keen anticipation of the end of time pressed in upon Frank and Florence. A rash of unexpected deaths in the church made personal commitment all the more pressing. And Florence, little knowing that she would have some fifty years of service still ahead of her, prayed only that she would be ready "whenever the Saviour might call," as she wrote in her long, descriptive letters to the folks at home.

She needed all the resources she had for the new avalanche of trials which next overtook her. In early 1931 twin problems arose for the family. Florence had been perfectly able to take Winton and Francis through their first eight grades. While she had taught English at the Armenian school, they had both attended classes there. After all, 2 + 2 makes 4 in Armenian, Turkish, Assyrian, Persian or English. The colorful array of languages even lent a certain glamor to the more somber aspects of mathematics.

Along with the book lessons, the boys learned industry and the management of money and time. They spent hours making doll furniture, picture frames, and jigsaw puzzles from dismantled wooden crates. They sold much of what they made, and from the proceeds Winton bought his first pair of long pants. Yes, the boys were growing up—the evidence was clear on every hand.

Florence's responsibilities grew in direct proportion to the church membership, it seemed. In addition to the old secretary-treasurership, she had added the Sabbath School department and the Dorcas work. Moreover, she continued to be the chief hostess, seeing to the housing, feeding, washing, and ironing for the many mission guests—some of whom arrived and stayed for weeks.

Her good health and indestructibility, which she had brought to Persia with her almost twenty years before as one of her greatest assets, had recently begun to fail her in an alarming and altogether discouraging way. Added to the migraine headaches which had plagued her for years, she developed a mysterious condition which the doctors variously diagnosed as "intercostal neuralgia," catarrh of the lungs, and tuberculosis. The real ailment had never quite been pinpointed up to this time, and the diathermy, X-ray, and ultra-violet ray treatments did little to relieve the intense pain that came with any little movement.

Sitting in an easy chair propped up with pillows, she heard the boys' lessons almost every day. For months a great black spot appeared on her lower back where the pain was worst. Then it faded away to a mottled area like marble.

Finally Dr. Hargreaves said, in the disconcerting manner which doctors are wont to assume under certain circumstances, "You can consider your days of usefulness numbered unless you get away from Persia and get some proper medical treatment."

The verdict could scarcely be ignored. The appearance of too many other oppressive symptoms made that impossible. Then the question of Winton's future loomed large. He needed to be in school. Florence, handicapped by illness, didn't feel equal to teaching high school subjects anyway. But how could a fourteen-year-old be sent halfway around the world to live in a dormitory with strangers?

In her dilemma, Florence gave consideration to the possibility which always lurks in the back of every missionary mind: "Is it time to move home to the States and give the boys a chance at a good school?" Then her faith would revive, and she would rebuke herself for the thought. "God has always opened up a way out of every trouble. He will this time too."

Absorbed in his work, Frank probably didn't realize the depths of discouragement to which Florence often fell during these years. Her loyalty forbade her complaining or laying more burdens on his already stooping shoulders.

The coming of A. E. Ashod from Istanbul to become the mission secretary-treasurer did relieve Florence of at least one portion of her responsibilities.

At this time the Olsons had a furlough due. Since they planned to travel through Europe en route to America, it seemed an opportune time for both of the Osters' prevailing problems to get attention at the same time. Florence would enter the sanitarium in Gland, Switzerland, and Winton could start school at Collonges, France. The two institutions were close enough together to allow reasonably frequent visits—for the encouragement of the young, first-time-away-from-home student and the comfort of the tired, lonely patient.

"Life's going to be bleak without you, Floss," Frank said, as he struggled with farewell words. He had never been a sentimental man—ever. "But it's for the best. Switzerland—it's still my home in a special way, you know." He smiled down on her. "It's beautiful and will surely bring you back to health soon."

"If it's God's will—" Florence began. She felt so tired—so very tired sometimes.

Before he slammed the taxi door shut, Frank bent for one more kiss. "Don't worry about the boys and me, Floss. Not for one minute. Just concentrate on getting well."

The long taxi journey took the travelers past the famous Bisitun rock with its tri-lingual inscription, which gave modern archaeology the key to many of the secrets of antiquity. After a brief stopover in Baghdad, they went on for 500 miles through the Syrian Desert, traveling at night to avoid the intense heat of the day. They stopped at the sole refreshment place, Rutba Wells, an oasis, and then headed toward Damascus.

At about midnight the taxi driver turned to Winton. "Can you drive?"

"Oh, yes, I know how to drive," he replied.

Florence could tell that he was trying to hide his eagerness. With the faithful old Chevrolet Frank had taught him good driving habits, so Florence didn't worry when he took the wheel. Certainly they couldn't afford to stop and waste the cool night hours.

As the man and boy exchanged places, the chauffeur pointed to the sky and said, "Do you see those two stars?"

Winton nodded, "Yes, I do."

"Good. Now just keep your eyes fixed on them and drive straight toward them. You shouldn't have any trouble." No road, as such, existed, but the time-honored resources of navigation, the stars, were still available, trusty as ever.

The driver slumped down into the front seat and almost immediantly fell into a heavy sleep. Winton, proudly at the wheel meanwhile, headed off for Damascus. He watched the stars intently at first—they never seemed to get any closer.

Some time later the chauffeur awoke and looked out the window. "Stop! Stop! Where are we?" He jumped out of the car to get his bearings. "Why didn't you follow the stars?"

"I did," Winton responded with heat. "But I couldn't just drive over the rocks and ditches, could I?"

"Whatever you did, you should always have watched the stars." The driver resumed his place behind the wheel.

"I did. See them, still up there?" Winton's adventure had begun to turn sour for sure.

"Those two stars are in the east, boy, and they lead back to Baghdad." The chauffeur swore softly and swung the car around with a jerk.

Winton's desert detour having been corrected, the party entered the Syrian port-of-entry, at sunrise. Because they had traveled through Basra where an epidemic of cholera raged, they had to go through health inspection. Everyone passed except Florence. "I guess I look so deteriorated that they just reject me on general principles," she sighed.

The Olsons took a hotel for the night, and Winton went with them; but he didn't stay long. Within an hour he was back at the door of the quarantine room where Florence had to spend the night. "Mother, I'm *not* leaving you here alone in this place."

That night they spent there together proved to be a busy one. The mosquitoes and fleas kept the hours wakeful. Florence kept shooing the creeping things off Winton. If she didn't have cholera already surely she would be a prime candidate for something worse.

In the morning, however, she finally received clearance and was allowed to join the rest of the party aboard the ship that would take them to Marseilles, France. From that point they scattered: Olsons to continue their furlough journey to the States; Winton to enroll at the Seminaire Adventiste at Collonges-sous-Salève, France; and Florence to be admitted to Lake Geneva Sanitarium, at Gland, Switzerland, overlooking Lake Geneva.

Frank had been right. If lovely landscapes could cure, surely she would have been healed the very first day she sat in a wheelchair on the lakeshore and looked across the clean, blue water to the soft, orchard-tufted hills along the edge. Persia lay in another world—far, far away.

That school year proved to be a difficult transition time for Winton. "Mom, I used to think I knew some French, but now—" He lapsed into uncertain silence. His career in the French school seemed to be undercut in much the same way that confidence in his navigational abilities had recently been shaken in the desert.

Florence patted him on the shoulder. "Keep courage, Winton. The good nun in Tabriz spent a good many hours tutoring you in French. I'm sure some of it took root. It'll come, dear."

"Well, I keep trying." Winton stood up to leave. He had several hours' journey back to Geneva, across the border, and up to the foot of the Salève. "By the way, Mom, the doctor says my new glasses will be ready next time I come down. Maybe that's going to help."

"It very well could." Florence reached up to kiss her handsome young teenager. It had been a source of relief to discover that he hadn't had trachoma after all. If Dr. Hargreaves had been around at that time, they'd have had much more skilled attention, Florence knew. But the doctor had been entitled to post-graduate study in England. And he had also gone to bring a bride back to Persia. A man needed a wife there, and Florence had felt happy for him.

As for Florence herself, the cure was nothing so simple as the prescription of glasses. It was diagnosed as a heavily ulcerated digestive tract.

In the dim twilight zone of post-surgery anesthesia, Florence became aware of Winton bending over her. "Mother's getting cold—she's sinking." Winton's voice had a sharp edge as he turned to the doctor.

Florence caught that note, even through her floating haze of pain. "Pray," she whispered. She had never known another word in extremity. It had served her through so many years and trials already that it now came as an automatic reaction quite outside of conscious decision.

Winton knelt by her bed and prayed the prayer which he had learned from babyhood—the one about God's will. And by the time he returned to Collonges the next day, he could be assured by the doctor that his mother would improve.

For Florence, however, the three-month recuperation was long and unsatisfying, the beauties of Lake Geneva notwithstanding. Sitting in her wheelchair on the lawn overlooking the lake was therapy indeed, but it also gave her too much time to dream of home in Tehran, which had become their home after their move from Tabriz. Frank's letters came regularly, telling the familiar story of mission work—the meetings, the itineraries, Francis' progress in school and his advanced skills with his hobbies. Yes, and he missed Winton too. But no mention was made of Kenneth. When Florence inquired of him, somehow the questions never got answered. Black specters of fear kept rising in her mind. Why was Kenneth never mentioned? Was he sick? Moments came when she ever imagined him already dead and buried. These visions terrified her hours, waking and sleeping. Frank, of course, would not want to shock her with bad news because of her own unresolved state of health. If mission worries had not finished her off, she decided, anxiety over her family would.

Finally after many weeks, when she had almost reached her breaking point, Frank wrote. "Kenneth has been sick with typhoid. We've had an anxious time, but he's on the mend now." So that was it!

Tension drained off, and Florence wept with relief for her baby's safety. He was still the baby in her mind, despite his seven years. She thought of Frank, alone through the crisis. Of course mission friends surrounded him, but she could see him during the long night hours nursing, loving, caring, and praying over Kenneth's bed. She should have been there beside him.

Her own case, however, remained at a standstill. Her prolonged illness with typhoid had weakened her considerably. The doctor felt it unwise to operate. After three months she transferred to the Cantonal Hospital in Geneva. When the medical staff there also reached the end of their resources a month later, she went north to the Waldfriede Sanitarium in Berlin. There her trouble was diagnosed as ulcerative colitis. Under the care of Dr. Conradi and his wife, she underwent further tests and treatments and, at last, surgery. Gradually her ulcerative colitis began to clear.

Now thoughts of getting home to Persia really obsessed her mind. Time dragged on, and her desire to leave became so strong that she could almost taste it! "All right, *Frau* Oster," the doctor said, as he surveyed her meditatively. "You do seem to be improving, but it's *still* against my better judgment. You will go now at your own risk."

"Oh, doctor, I will be so careful!" Florence's heart leaped to meet the happy words, "go now." The rest she heard only as an echo. Home to Frank and the boys. Yes, she would pay any price for that now.

"And after such heavy abdominal surgery, you must not lift any luggage," the doctor's voice tuned in from the echo, and she heard him plainly. "You must *not* under any circumstances carry anything heavy for at least another six weeks."

Those conditions seemed reasonable and certainly easy enough to meet, Florence thought. So, in a whirl of school-girl excitement, she prepared for departure, telegraphing the good news to Frank in Tabriz. Winton remained behind in Collonges. He had now mastered French, conquered his environment completely, and carried off top grades in his classes. "Our first fledgling has left the nest," Florence thought, as she headed back toward Persia alone.

She chose to go through Russia, not for convenience certainly, but because it offered the shortest route. Having joined a fairly large party of tourists she anticipated not only a degree of comfort but also minimal obstacles at the borders.

Upon reaching the border between Poland and Russia, Florence remembered border crossings of other years. But being without Frank this time, the customs ordeal seemed even worse than before. Every piece of baggage of every person had to be thoroughly examined. Florence was among the last in line. Then the official discovered her little Bible in her handbag. "Hah, hah! Ho, ho! Come here!" The customs officers crowded around, apparently overcome with hilarity. "Here's a woman who has a Bible!"

When the general mirth had subsided, the officer headed into an inner office with the precious Bible. "Oh, please don't take my Bible away!" Florence felt sick with fear, remembering how it had been her daily, even hourly, companion during the long months of illness and anxiety. "I need it."

"Then, get another somewhere else," the man said.

"But that one is special to me," Florence pleaded. "I've been sick for so long, and that one has been my special companion."

Finally the officials consented, but they put the Bible into one of her suitcases and put a government seal on it. "All right then, if you must. But don't let this seal be broken when you leave Russia, or it will be the worse for you. Bibles are not read in Russia."

By now Florence was indeed the very last to board the train. "Please, sir," she asked. "May I have a porter to put my luggage on the train?"

"Hah, hah! A porter!" The laughter broke out again, re-echoing in the rafters of the customhouse. "You have a God, don't you? Let Him help you! Ho, ho!"

Amid the laughter Florence surveyed her bags. Everyone else was already on the train. "Pray!" What else?

She had no more than put the thought together and sent it heavenward than a tall young man strode down the platform toward her. She said nothing, for the situation formulated itself so suddenly she had no time. But when she motioned toward her suitcases, he picked them up immediately.

The train had begun to move along the platform as he hoisted the bags onto the platform of the last car. Then, with a strong arm, he helped Florence up onto the steps of the car, which was gathering speed. In the same moment she slipped him a couple of *rubles* (about $1), and he was gone.

Too weak and upset to go directly into the carriage, she sat down on the steps to summon her strength and calm her nerves. She hung onto the handrail with one hand and the luggage with the other, as the train chugged away from the station.

Then she caught sight of one of the men who had mocked her God. She—or more correctly God—would have the last word after all. "There, you see," she called to him, "My God *did* help me!"

One of the In-tourist passengers heard her call and came out to the back platform, where she and her luggage sat huddled together on the steps. "Here, let me help you find a seat," the man said.

Florence sat back at last, suitcases stowed in the rack above and under the seat. She had not lifted them. As the forests of western Russia began to stretch out on the rolling meadows, her mind strayed back to her long months of illness and forward to her family. But most of all, just now, she thought of that tall young man. "Who was he? From where had he come? To where had he gone?"

"Dear Lord," Florence murmured to herself, overawed at the thought. "Surely, I'm not worthy! But was he—was he perhaps—an angel? Sent to rescue me? *Me*?" The marvelous thought kept moving around and around in her mind. Whatever it was, it kept her heart warm and light all the way to Baku.

As soon as she had boarded the boat for crossing the Caspian Sea, she broke the Russian seal on her suitcase. "They didn't really control anything after all," she said, smiling to herself as she took out her Bible. The little cabin just didn't seem large enough to contain her happiness and gratitude. Her joy climaxed the next day when the ship docked in the Persian port of Pahlevi and there she saw Frank, Francis, and Kenneth standing on the wharf waiting for her.

Surely Francis had grown at least two inches. Kenneth still looked a little pale and pinched from his bout with typhoid. And Frank, dear Frank! He looked his same steady, loving self.

Florence's enforced detour had lasted eight months.

Tests—the Small and the Great

Mission routines with visitors at home and exhausting itineraries all through Azerbaijan quickly resumed for Florence. Quality hotel accommodations had not made the rapid progress that other phases of Persian culture had achieved. Many nights still had to be spent in *caravansaries* or in little rooms atop garages—the twentieth century version of the old desert caravan stops, with the camels replaced by trucks and wagons.

Frank and Florence had learned right from the start that the only way to be sure of a clean bed was to carry their own folding cots and bedding. Frank had devised an ingenious method for outwitting most of the insects—except for the jumping fleas. He set each leg of the cots in a cup of water—a procedure which baffled the ordinary, more naive bugs that swarmed over the mud floors. But not the bedbugs—they vexed the Osters constantly.

"For the life of me," Frank declared one night as he set out the leg-cups for the cots, "I don't see how they get past the water. "I *know* they can't swim."

"They must be the intelligentsia of the pest population," Florence said. "If we get more bites, though, we'll have sores as bad as the *salaks* we've had before." She dreaded the thought of those ugly, oozy sores she had treated for months at a stretch on the boys, Frank, and herself too. Everyone who came to Tehran seemed destined to get the sandfly bites. Florence remembered the time poor Francis had thirteen of them on his face at one time, all of which took a full year to run their course and dry up.

In Persia, it seemed, nothing just went away because you waited. Things very often got much worse before they got better. And insect bite could become a major problem.

"Anyway," Frank went on, "I'm going to watch those bedbugs tonight and see how they do it."

In the flickering lamplight, he waited until his patience was rewarded. He saw the bugs climb the walls and trek across the ceiling. Then they dropped down on his cot. "There, Floss!" He reached over to be sure she was awake. "I saw them do it! They walked across the ceiling and dropped on our cots from there. They plan it!" he marveled.

Although equally amazed, Florence thought it really seemed like altogether too much know-how for a bedbug. "Perhaps the ones that fell down were already up there in the dirty matting in the ceiling," she ventured.

"That could be," Frank conceded, as he put out the lantern. "But I'd still like to know for sure."

"Well, enough research for one night," Florence yawned. "Let's sleep as best we can."

One journey to Hamadan a few months later, however, put the bedbugs, predatory as they were, quite into the shade. The Osters had just gotten into bed in the simple hotel room they had rented, when Florence screamed and clutched Frank by the arm. "Look! A snake!"

And there it was, head weaving tentatively out of the matting between the rafters overhead. Galvanized into motion by the shock, Frank leaped out of bed and onto the floor in one movement. "And there's another!" Florence grabbed at him again. Sure enough, another snake had worked its way out of the opposite corner. And another! And another!

Frank opened the door and called, "*Zood bin inja, pesar* [Come quickly, boy]. Come quickly. This room's full of snakes." He armed himself with a stick he found propped up behind a wooden chest under the window.

The servant came on the run, not to kill the snakes but to save them. "No, no, *Agha!*" He restrained Frank from striking at a serpent almost fully extended over the door frame. Florence looked on, clutching the blanket up to her chin, unable to let out even one more scream. "We want the snakes to stay here," the man said.

"To *stay* here!" Florence repeated the incomprehensible words, still in shock.

"Yes, of course, *Agha,*" the servant went on. "We've trained the snakes to kill the rats and mice. And we have none of those in our place here," he added proudly.

"But how can we sleep here with the snakes in the room? Won't they—?"

"Have no fear, *Agha,*" the man soothed. "The snakes are harmless and very friendly. When all is quiet, they also will sleep. You will see." And with that the champion of the reptiles retired, leaving Frank, Florence and the snakes to work matters out by mutual agreement.

"Well, Floss," Frank climbed into bed again. "There seems to be nothing more to do. We can't find another place to sleep at this time of night."

"All right, we'll stay then." Florence moved over a little closer for safety. At least a snake oughtn't to come between them. "And for once," she added, "we have positive assurance that no rats or mice will trouble us."

"Ah, yes." Frank laughed and snuggled well down into the blankets. "It's a great comfort to know that. I feel so relieved!"

When the Osters departed in the morning, they left a quiet and apparently snakeless room. Perhaps the reptiles had found another place to forage for refreshments in the course of the night, perhaps a hitherto unvisited colony of mice or rats.

On another night some months later, back at home in Tabriz, the routines of life splintered apart in one dreadful hour, well past midnight. A violent earthquake catapulted the Osters out of bed. Francis and Kenneth came running from their room in terror. While the walls swayed and dishes clattered off the shelves, they all crawled on hands and knees to the door. The wooden beams somehow held up the heavy mud-and-straw roof. The compound filled with other startled escapees, and all gathered in the garden to spend the rest of the night under the stars.

Morning news indicated that although Tabriz received relatively light shocks, the nearby district of Salmas had been entirely destroyed, with great loss of life. Frank and Melcom Gasparian, who by now had become Frank's right-hand man, immediately loaded the Chevrolet to the roof with *lavash* and other food supplies. Trip after trip they made, driving across the shattered earthquake zones, offering relief to the thousands who had nothing to eat.

"You'd never believe it, Floss," Frank said one night as he watched Florence and some of the women get another massive *lavash* baking session under way. "This afternoon we found an old couple sitting together on a log. They said it had been the beam of their house."

"The poor people! Had they saved anything?" Florence asked.

"Nothing," Frank replied, "except for an old teakettle they had there between them. Everything else was rubble. You couldn't identify a single item in the whole mess."

The tremors continued for two months, and people slept outdoors rather than run the very real risk of having the mud walls fall on them in the event of another quake. Some twenty families brought their rugs and mats and camped in the spacious yard of the mission compound. So the Osters had plenty of company for all those many nights outdoors. The children enjoyed it all as a long, continued picnic and camp-out.

The scorpions, however, took advantage of the emergency situation to prey upon the sleepers. The pale yellow scorpions were comparatively harmless, although their crawly, scaly appearance was repulsive enough. The black ones, on the other hand, stung with a deadly poison which could cause excruciating pain, prolonged sickness, and even death.

One night after another series of earth tremors had confirmed in everyone's mind that it still wasn't safe to return to the houses, Florence found herself in another kind of danger. She felt it first on her leg, just below the knee—the sickening sensation of many little feet walking northward, up her thigh and across her stomach. "Frank! Frank!" She heard her voice, a kind of hoarse croak that didn't sound like her at all. "Something's crawling up under my nightgown! I think it's a scorpion."

Frank stiffened. "Don't move, Floss." His fingers reached for hers, but nothing else stirred. "A scorpion won't sting unless it's attacked. Don't move."

"Yes, Frank," Florence hissed between her teeth. The scorpion now traveled up her neck and over her chin. By sheer will power she held herself tense, while a cold sweat broke out all over her. Now across her nose and onto her forehead. Then, with a slight plunk, she heard it drop on the pillow by her ear.

Meanwhile, Frank had edged out of bed and struck a match.

When the huge black scorpion reached the edge of the mattress, Frank flicked it off onto the ground and smashed it with his shoe. Eventually Florence stopped trembling, but then she dozed off into a nightmare filled with black scorpions.

In the morning Francis and Kenneth studied the great scorpion with an interest worthy of the most dedicated zoologist. The "scorpion season" following the great earthquake gave them the chance to pursue their research quite productively.

One day they found a scorpion which they imprisoned in a little box full of wood shavings from their jig-saw, and then they set fire to the shavings. The scorpion searched for a way of escape through the wall of fire, but found none. Then, in the best tradition of dramatic heroism, he took his stand in the center of the ring of fire, arched his tail, and stung himself on his own head. In a few seconds he fell over dead.

The suicide depressed the boys temporarily, for it was not wholly without its sadness. "Yes, it really was too bad for the poor scorpion," Florence agreed when they told her the story. "But they are so deadly, it was for the best. Do you remember how that lady over at the Presbyterian mission was so sick for three months and nearly died after the black scorpion stung her?"

When Francis turned sixteen, it was time—more than time—to consider getting him off to school in the States. Dreams came full and rosy, with Francis as excited as any fellow in his circumstances might dare to be.

When he had his physical examination, however, the doctor found that he had trachoma again. The six months required for the painful treatments with the "hell-stone" brought an immediate halt to all plans. Then, when that ordeal had almost finished, he began running a constant fever of 100-102°. "I have such queer pains and aches everywhere, Mom," he sighed.

"Undulant fever," the doctors finally decided. The days slipped on through the fall of 1934, and on past Christmas. Hopes of going to school in the States shimmered in the far-off distance like a desert mirage, and Francis tried to wait patiently. Finally at the end of February Florence could announce the good news to the family at home. "At last, Francis is out of bed!"

Frank now wrote to the General Conference requesting a furlough for Florence and the boys. He would stay by the mission, but it seemed reasonable that after all the sickness the family should have some time at home. When the request was turned down, however, Francis had to make plans for a solo departure.

Meanwhile, Winton, their eldest, was on the eve of graduating from Indiana Academy. After two years at Collonges, he had returned to the states to Uncle Omer and Aunt Lulu Butler to finish grade twelve. Now he was ready to begin the required two years of pre-medicine at Emmanuel Missionary College. So Francis would take his place as "resident nephew" in the Butler home.

Francis traveled home with Presbyterian missionary friends. Florence watched the train leave Tehran with Francis at the window, and she dabbed away at her eyes. Only one boy left now. Mission service, at times like this, seemed to have an inordinately high price tag on it.

Letters soon demonstrated that, for Francis, it had all been for the best. Winton played the part of big brother admirably, advising his inexperienced, Persian-reared brother on all the niceties of life in the States. "And right from where you are now, in grade ten, study hard and make the honor roll," brother Winton admonished.

Francis had to admit that all this seemed a pretty big responsibility.

"Of course, you don't plan to do it in your own strength," Winton advised. "No matter how busy you get, take time to pray, and God will help you every time, I know."

Florence and Frank laughed and wept over the letters. Yes, Francis made the honor roll the first term—Winton's prescription worked. Also he became the baritone in the academy male quartet. Above and beyond all, he just couldn't believe what it could be like being among so many Adventists, in one place. By proxy the boys' triumphs and good times were relived in the mission house in Tehran.

In February, 1936, Frank received a letter from the General Conference appointing him as a delegate to represent the Middle East and Central European Divisons at the forthcoming session in San Francisco.

"Oh, Frank," Florence exclaimed. "That will mean we can see the boys and all the family again." After all, their last furlough was now more than six years behind them.

Frank frowned, running his eye down the letter again. "I can't understand. It doesn't even mention you and Kenneth."

Florence stared in disbelief. "But surely the General Conference session would mean furlough. It almost always does, doesn't it?" She grasped at any hope—any precedent.

Frank wrote a letter that night to the division office requesting furlough for the rest of the family. He himself had been granted two-and-a-half months, including travel time. Not much, but at least he could see the boys.

Florence hung on, hoping for good news from the office; but when it arrived at last, it was more frustrating than no news at all. No committee action could be taken on furloughs now because personnel had already dispersed, headed for San Francisco.

When it was time for Frank to leave, Florence's spirits fell flat—further down than at any time in all the twenty-three years since she had arrived in Persia. She couldn't shake off the depression. Mission responsibility, Kenneth's needs, a hundred tasks kept her busy—as far as that went. Still, she fought discouragement hourly, and also it had been a bad winter—more colitis and three bouts with malaria. A tiredness of the spirit, not the body alone, sapped her strength.

"Why couldn't I just die and rest until Jesus comes," she wondered some days. Then other days were different. She thought of the boys, of Frank, and of the great cause for which they had given the best years of their lives. On those days she wanted to live.

The first week of June brought sudden change. A cable from Frank in Washington, D. C. told her to come—they would have a furlough after all! Florence's excitement over that information, however, was much tempered by other news. Francis had been very ill for twenty-two days. While out singing with his quartet on a tour of churches, he had caught cold. Pneumonia followed, and his low resistance from the long siege with undulant fever left him defenseless. Winton had left his summer colporteuring of medical books in Quebec, Canada, to come down and be with his brother.

Continually dogged by sickness! Florence wondered how it all could ever "work together for good." Amid all these uncertainties, torn between hope and despair, joy and depression, Florence hurried through the preparations for their departure—hers and Kenneth's.

Passports and visas! Then permission to take money out of the country. The regular forty dollars allowed would hardly see them all the way to Indiana. When her application was denied, Florence got an advance of money from a faithful church member in Baghdad. The Nairn Bus Company now replaced the star-guided car convoys across the Syrian Desert. On to Damascus, Beirut, and a boat to southern Italy. Then in Naples, Florence found a swift ship, the *S. S. Rex,* going directly to New York.

No sightseeing, no detours this time. Florence's mind remained fixed on but one point—Francis lying sick in bed. Her boy needed her. The long Atlantic crossing gave time for much thought and prayer. No letters could reach her now, but she constantly held before the Lord her son, to whom her heart reached out across the ocean. The last message she had received in Iran indicated that Francis was improving—news which enabled her to endure that long journey half way around the world.

The arrival in New York differed from the last furlough in many ways. The anxieties which enveloped her almost eradicated the memory of that last entry—the five of them with a whole happy year spread out before them.

Although she expected no one, Florence stood with Kenneth on an upper deck surveying the welcoming crowds on the wharf below. The ship eased into its moorings, and Kenneth grabbed her arm. "Mom! Mom! There's Daddy down there!"

He stood in the sober, ministerial suit he always favored, gazing up at them steadfastly. Florence's first pang of joy at seeing him changed instantly to fear. Why wasn't he in San Francisco at the General Conference session? Or why wasn't he with Francis? Why had he come clear to New York to meet them?

Finally, they walked down the gangplank and into speaking range—then the enormity of the truth dawned on them. "How's Francis?" Florence had to speak that question.

Frank stepped forward and took her into his arms. "Don't ask me, Floss." He strained her to him. "Don't ask, my dear one." With that first rush of grief piercing through her there on the New York dock, Florence knew the answer.

As they rode in broken silence to the Times Square Hotel, the story came out bit by bit. Francis had been buried two weeks ago in the Byington and White plot in the Oak Hill Cemetery in Battle

Creek. Florence and Kenneth had come too late, though they had traveled as fast as was humanly possible.

That first evening together in the impersonal hotel passed in tears, prayers, and piecing together the story of Francis' last days. "I received the message in San Francisco and came back to Cicero immediately," Frank said. "After he came out of the hospital we had so many ups and downs—we lived between hope and despair for days."

Francis had put up a valiant fight for life. Perhaps Indiana Academy had never had a pupil with more zest for living. When the doctor said that the end was only a matter of time, the family gathered around him in his last hours of consciousness. Through more than 100 hours in a coma, his courageous young heart beat on, as he grasped for the life which had eluded him so early. Late in the evening on July 1, 1936, he died.

"The family—Frank, we should—" Florence's voice sounded hollow, far beyond tears.

"Don't worry about it now, Floss. I wrote to them all about it the day after he died. They know." Frank put his arm around her as they sat together on the bed. "There's something in all of this for which we can praise God."

"What's that?" Florence knew that there were many things, no doubt, but just now she had to grope to think of even one.

"I had many good conversations at his bedside," Frank said. "He was thoroughly resigned to live or die, according to God's will for him. He sought out every wrong to make it right."

"Bless his heart," Florence sobbed now. "*Inshallah*—"how well Francis had learned the meaning of those words. How well—and how young.

Frank went on with his story. "He always begged us to have worship together in his room, and often I found him praying alone. Even when words were almost beyond him, he would still whisper, "O Lord God, Thou knowest—"

Finally, worn out by travel and the stress of the last hours, Kenneth and Frank fell asleep. Florence listened to the traffic in the streets far below—the traffic which seemed to go on forever. Sleep wouldn't come. She craved the assurance that her bright, life-loving teenager had truly been ready to die. "Lord, I need a promise," she said.

Taking her worn little Bible which had seen her through her testing time in Switzerland and Germany—the one that had been scorned by the Russian atheists—she went into the bathroom and turned on the light. "Lead me directly to the right verse," she prayed. She opened the book and her finger fell on Isaiah 43:1, ". . . Fear not, for I have redeemed thee, I have called thee by my name; thou are mine." An almost audible voice said, "Don't stop here, read verse 2." She went on: "When thou passest through the waters, I will be with thee . . . when thou walkest through fire, thou shalt not be burned."

Florence knew that she had found *her* promise, and the miracle of that moment has never left her. It was as if the prophet had looked down the centuries, right into the heartbreak of her family there in the Times Square Hotel. The fires of grief and the floods of sorrow that she had walked through— She looked at verse 5, again almost as if by audible instruction: "Fear not . . . I will bring thy seed from the east, and gather thee from the west." Yes, baby Winona back in the east, and now Francis in the west—but the resurrection day would gather them all together once more. On the strength of that, she *could* go on.

"Dear God, according to the will and the strength Thou givest me—" And so Florence prayed peace back into her heart. She stood up, switched off the light, and returned to bed and sleep. At dawn she rose with Frank, ready to face another day.

"Frank," she said, as they prepared to go out for breakfast, "God gave me assurances about Francis last night. Now I feel that I can sincerely thank God for the seventeen precious years we had him and not complain and become bitter over asking the question 'Why?' "

"My own Floss!" Frank held her close. "In those last days I spent with our boy, I felt the same assurances, and I told God that I could accept death for him, if He saw it within His purpose." He looked deep into her eyes, which had held so many tears in recent years. "Now we'll go on together." And so, in the strength of those promises and commitments, Florence and Frank walked out hand in hand to start their third furlough.

Call to Turkey

Even faith and dedication, of course, didn't spare the Osters the pangs of sorrow and depression. Frank and Florence had to work and pray their way through their whole cycle of grief as they prepared to return to Persia for the fourth time. Frank went first, and Florence followed at the end of the 1937 school year at Emmanuel Missionary College.

"In a way, we're back where we started twenty-four years ago, Floss," Frank remarked.

"That's right. Just the two of us alone again," Florence answered. Kenneth had been left behind this last time, to follow his brothers' course through Indiana Academy and on to college in Berrien Springs. She couldn't help thinking again how family separations came very much too early to families in overseas service.

As the months went by, however, news poured in from home—news that Florence would very much like to have been part of. Winton had been accepted at the College of Medical Evangelists at Loma Linda. He still rode high on that same inspiration with which Dr. Hargreaves had motivated him so many years before. Kenneth graduated from Indiana Academy and dedicated himself to following in the footsteps of his missionary father—a fact which brought Frank a great pleasure which he couldn't easily disguise. Then, in June, 1938, Winton married Dorothy Wier, a girl he had had on his mind—and now, obviously, also in his heart—ever since academy days in Indiana.

Florence spent some time dreaming over that letter. "I would *love* to be there in Hinsdale, right this minute," she said aloud.

Frank looked up surprised. "Oh, the wedding. Yes, we ought to be there, Floss; but instead we're here."

Florence didn't say any more. A matter-of-fact man probably could never really understand the importance of a woman's being present at a family wedding ceremony. She read the letter all over again, just to indulge herself in a little more wishful thinking for at least a few hours. Grandfather White would be conducting the service too—which brought to mind another wedding in London. Dear Frank! What a life they'd had together these twenty-five years. The mission work had moved from pioneer "zero" conditions to a stable, consolidated mission with a competent staff of national and European workers. Deprivation, yes, but also rewards that could never be estimated in material terms.

The twenty-seventh anniversary of Frank's entry into Persia had almost arrived when a letter came from the Central European Division—a letter which would have far-reaching effects on the Oster's next six years of service. "Floss, here's a letter from the brethren. You'd better sit down to hear it."

Obediently she sat down. "What are we going to do next?" Florence had learned to live with the unexpected so long that she didn't try to imagine what this would be.

"They're asking us to move to Turkey," Frank said.

"Turkey? To leave Persia?" Florence turned this around in her mind. Something different—to be sure. The reasons, on the other hand, were self-evident. She knew that the Seventh-day Adventist churches in Turkey had been closed for the past seven years. Frank's pioneer experience in Iran and his command of the Turkish language, albeit a different dialect, had encouraged the division committee to think that he might succeed where all else had failed in Turkey.

"It's not going to be easy, Floss," Frank said. "When I was in Istanbul two years ago, the members of the church warned me against standing while speaking, and against kneeling for prayer—because of the spies."

"No, it won't be easy. But when have we ever had anything easy, Frank?" Florence could remember the leisurely tour through Europe in 1928, the classes she had attended at Emmanuel Missionary College—a few things like that. But easy? No!

"Are you sorry, Floss?" Frank looked at her, his eyes framing a question far larger than his words had spoken.

"Sorry? Never, Frank!" Florence could read his uncertainties about the move, the weariness of hard living, and much more in his tired face. "No, I'd do it—we'd do it—all again, the very same way."

They started out immediately to visit all the churches and companies in Persia on one last grand itinerary, all the way from Isfahan in the south to the Caspian Sea in the north. Then they sold off their household goods.

The journey from Tehran to Ankara provided an unusually large variety of incidents to make their departure the more memorable. The 425 miles from the capital to Tabriz took a little more than a day and was accomplished in a crowded, rented car. Fortunately none of the eight passengers nor the driver was hurt when they collided with a truck. It took a hammer, crowbar, and a large measure of patience, however, to separate the front left fender from the wheel so they could go on.

The week spent visiting the many friends and church members in Tabriz provided an interlude which they would need. They paid for two places in the cab of a truck, at fifty tomans (fifty dollars) apiece. Prudent and thrifty as ever, Frank just couldn't be reconciled to paying 300 tomans for a car. "We would not spend the church's money on that luxury, Floss," he said. "We'll manage."

They did manage, but with effort. For five days they sat jammed into the truck cab with three other passengers, plus the driver. The freight consisted of the salted intestines of certain unidentified but long-dead animals, being shipped to Germany for sausage-making. Fifteen passengers crouched atop the twenty-five barrels of odiferous intestines, and the driver and his helper tied everyone's baggage securely on the roof. A terrible stench enveloped the whole vehicle. "That meat will really be ripe by the time it gets to Germany," Frank speculated.

"Makes us glad to be vegetarian doesn't it?" Florence replied with a grimace.

The first night the Osters had a room to themselves. They pulled the benches away from the mud walls and lay down to sleep on them, remembering the driver's injunction, "We leave in the morning at 4 o'clock promptly. Whoever is not there will be left behind."

Accordingly, the whole company turned out ready to travel, long before dawn. Prolonged sleeping in the filthy room held no attractions for Frank and Florence anyway. The driver and his friend, however, failed to appear. Hours passed, and their room remained closed! Had there been foul play, Florence wondered. Finally, in the late afternoon, the men sauntered forth, trailed by a bedraggled looking woman who had enlivened the night for them. Although neither man looked fit for the responsibilities of driving, the journey recommenced anyway.

The second night the Osters had a room with three beds in it—real beds. "Are the sheets clean?" Frank inquired.

"Oh, yes, *Agha*. Nice and clean. Perfect condition," the innkeeper affirmed.

A very cursory examination, however, proved that the beds had been occupied by perhaps dozens of people since the last washing. "I don't want to lie down here, Frank." Florence stood looking at the beds with loathing and a nauseous twist in her stomach.

"What do you want to do then?" Frank stretched out on the one nearest the door. "I'm tired."

Florence stood, still undecided—until a shower of bedbugs enveloped them. "Dear me! They didn't even wait for us to get the light out," she exclaimed.

Frank leaped into an upright position. "You're right, Floss. This won't do." They spent the rest of the night sleeping on some packing boxes out in the yard.

The next evening the truck reached the border and passed Persian customs. At two a.m. they got to Turkish customs and slept outside all the rest of that night. Since they had only a few suitcases, the Osters' passage through customs turned out to be fairly uneventful. Most of their things had been sent to Turkey by freight. They traveled on now in the hope of seeing their belongings again at some happy time in the future.

On the fourth day the truck had another late start, detained for causes similar to those of the first night. About eight miles down the road, they reached another customhouse, where the barrels of intestines had to undergo investigation. The passengers waited while the driver attended to his business—which included drinking enough liquor to keep his courage up. Eight hours later, near sundown, they were on their way again.

The terrible roads and now the utter darkness kept them all in a state of terror and suspense. Would the truck turn over? It was certainly overloaded, and the ruts in the road were deep. At every turn or bend the driver would yell rudely, "*An taraf beravid! Boro oon var* [Get over! Move over]!" But to get over was impossible. What a relief to get to a village at midnight and have the driver stop the truck. "We sleep here!" he shouted.

Florence surveyed the mud-walled huts clustering along the road. "There's no need to look for beds, Frank," she sighed. "They'd be just too filthy."

Frank studied the teahouse across the road intently. "I know what we can do! Let's ask the owner of that place to allow us to sleep on his roof."

"That sounds like a good idea," affirmed one of the other cab passengers.

And so it was arranged. Two other passengers who recognized the brilliance of Frank's idea also decided to sleep on the roof. "But wait, Frank. One more thing." Florence looked at the height with apprehension. "With no stairway and no ladder, how am I supposed to get up there?" The two men had already shinnied up one of the veranda poles, but Florence knew she couldn't manage that.

Frank brought a table out from the teahouse, set it under the eaves, and climbed up onto it. "Up you come, Floss!"

Florence found climbing onto the table a challenge in itself, for it swayed ominously with both of them on it. Then Frank picked her up lightly and hoisted her up over the edge of the roof. She could just get her elbows over the edge, when she felt all support fall away. A splintering of wood, a thud, and a rapidly receding cry from Frank—and she remained dangling in mid-air. The table had collapsed in a heap with Frank in its midst. Eager hands reached from above and hauled Florence up onto the roof. What a blessing that the two men had gone up first.

When Frank had picked himself up, settled for damages with the proprietor, and gathered up some of his dignity again, he climbed up the corner post in the safe, athletic way. With a fresh new rug under them—that was a surprise—they slept remarkably well under the stars that night.

Late on the fifth day the grotesque truckload of bone-weary people reached Erzerum—a point only two-thirds of the way to their destination. The smell of the intestines had grown in potency by the hour. Many of the "rear compartment" passengers had been sick all of the way, whether from the intestines or from the axle-deep ruts in the road, no one could tell. It made little difference, however, for they vomited all the way anyhow.

That night Frank found a good hotel. Florence and he reveled in the luxury of a bath and the opportunity to rid themselves of all the hoppers and creepers—the living creatures they had acquired over the past five days. During all that time they had no opportunity to take off their clothes, much less find clean ones.

The next morning Frank reached a decision. "We'll stay here and rest for the day and then find a car to take us the rest of the way."

"Oh Frank, I'm so glad. I'm sure the Lord will approve of our spending the extra money to finish up the journey. I really think we've economized enough for one time."

Frank looked repentant. "I'm so sorry, Floss. It really was too much. I had no idea—"

"Don't worry about it, Frank. It's past now, and nothing has befallen us but what rest and a little laundering will cure."

"But such a mistake! After twenty-seven years I should have known better than to try such a cheap ride." He shook his head in wonderment at his own gullibility. "We didn't even bring our folding cots. How could I have been so stupid!"

Poor Frank—he always had things so well in hand! Florence laughed. "Yes, it was a cheap ride—cheap in every possible way. But, never mind. We'll just chalk it up to experience—to last us for the *next* twenty-seven years!"

The truck driver stormed and ranted when the Osters abandoned his bargain-price tour into Turkey. Frank stood firm on the matter, however, and hired a good private car. Sitting in ease in the back seat while traveling through the lovely mountains of eastern Turkey was a luxury which could be fully enjoyed only by such as Frank and Florence. Especially after they had just spent five days crammed into a truck cab with four other people and careening through hundreds of miles of sheep and goat country—to say nothing of the nights!

In Trebazon they encountered some of their fellow-passengers from the truck, looking somewhat more used up than the last time they had seen them. "The second day after you left us in Erzerum, *Agha,*" one of the men said, "the truck turned over."

"Oh!" Florence's heart went out to those poor women on the back who had been so continuously sick. "Were any people hurt?"

"Yes, some, *Khanoom*. Some had to go to the hospital."

"And it was also unfortunate," added the other man, "because the sheep intestines got scattered all over the road."

Florence had to smile in spite of herself. She could see the mess, hear the driver, and smell the stench. Thank God, they had missed that episode.

"I suppose," Frank muttered in an aside to Florence, "that Germany's going to be a little short of sausage makings for a while."

After a day's rest in Trebazon, they took a boat for Samson, spending two days on the Black Sea to negotiate the 200 miles. Then, an uneventful train journey put them in Ankara.

The division committee had requested the Osters to live in the capital—the central inland city of Ankara—where there were no Seventh-day Adventists. It would be a new start. For the first few weeks before they found a little apartment, they lived in a tiny hotel room. They ate breakfasts and suppers there and went out for a warm meal at noon.

"I'm sorry, Frank, that I can't provide you a more varied menu." Florence came back from the lobby with their thermos bottle filled with hot water. "But facilities *are* limited." She mixed cocoa with a few drops of condensed milk. At seventy-five cents for a tiny can, the milk certainly couldn't be used recklessly. Nor could the precious malted milk tablets Vandella had given them. She had dispensed them carefully for months, and now they provided a prime source of nourishment. The hot drink and bread was often all they could find to eat.

Although the first Seventh-day Adventist worker had entered Turkey in 1889, the work had experienced many ups and downs. War, famine, and pestilence had brought many of the early church members to martyrdom and deportation. Now Frank and Florence surveyed their field. Precisely what could they do within the stringent restrictions laid upon them?

Religious freedom was certified to exist—one could believe anything he wanted. But the strings attached were complicated and full of hard knots. It was against the law to: speak to anyone about Christianity, to hand out a tract, to hold a meeting (public or private), to give away a Bible, to leave your city without notifying the police, or to move from one apartment to another without reporting to the police.

The questions never ended. "What is your work?"

"A teacher," Frank would reply.

"What do you teach?" he was then asked.

He and Florence puzzled over the replies that could be made to that one. An income tax also had to be paid, but if the source of their income were known to be a mission board they would be deported immediately. And to top it all, not one known Christian had been allowed to remain in the interior of the country.

The modernizing reforms of President Ataturk, who had overthrown the preceding sultan, matched those of Reza Shah Pahlavi of Iran in drama and culture—a shattering force. Still, they boded no good for Christian missions. The tiny Adventist congregation in Istanbul had lost even their small privilege of meeting weekly in the basement of a Protestant church.

"It's a straight-jacket, Floss!" Frank had spent another evening wrestling with the insolubles that faced them on every side. "I'm going to try to get Dr. Jean Nussbaum over here to loosen up a few of the bonds."

Dr. Nussbaum, the Religious Liberty Secretary for the Southern European Division, had to make two trips from Paris to meet all the right people and negotiate with government officials, before permission finally came through. The Adventists could go back to meeting in the basement of the church!

Florence never forgot that first glorious meeting together. Who ever could count it anything but a privilege to attend a public meeting? Absenteeism? Never! The believers in Turkey *knew*. And on that first Sabbath when the little company sang the doxology together, Florence thought she had never heard such fervor. Surely the praises went directly up to the throne of God Himself. And probably *He* hadn't heard anything like it for a while either.

In January 1939, after six months in their comfortable but restricted apartment in Ankara, Frank got an invitation to attend important union meetings convening in Alexandria. At the last moment he found a renter for their home. "Surprise, Floss. With the rent money, I can take you to Egypt with me." Florence remembered only too well being left behind at furlough time. How good of Frank to make sure she could go now, even if it had to be by "unpaid invitation."

Once out of Turkey, Florence could feel free to write as she wished. Folks at home got filled in now on information which otherwise would have been too risky to tell. Even private lessons of any kind, taught at home, could be given only by government permission; and that seemed impossible to obtain.

In Egypt Frank and Florence continued what had become an ongoing dialogue over the past months. "Surely, Frank," Florence would say, "probation must have closed for the Turks already. The way things are set up now, it's impossible to do anything in that country."

"It's not for us to set probation, Floss. But God must have brought us there for *some* reason," Frank remonstrated. "Maybe something will change here at these meetings."

"What good would that do? Nothing done here will affect the Turkish government," Florence responded, her courage diminishing again. And in the back of her mind, there inevitably arose that other idea. They could, after all these years, be back home in America with their boys, serving God even better than in law-bound Turkey.

Frank seemed as full of faith as Florence was of fears. Yet she knew, in those long hours when he lost himself in thought and prayer, that he too sometimes became afraid—although he always tried not to show it. Both agreed on one point—they would not shirk duty, and they wanted to be only in the place that God had designed for them at any given time. On that they agreed. Still, they differed strongly on the point of service in Turkey.

The Cairo meetings, meanwhile, proved to be pleasant and relaxing for both of them, especially after the many months of tension and anxiety. Florence hung on every word of Elder H. L. Rudy's devotional talks. The vigorous plans for expansion in the Arabic Union Missions (now the Middle East Union) brought the stimulus and motivation she needed just then too.

And now the brethren generally agreed that the Ankara experiment had not been productive and that the Osters should move to Istanbul, where at least they could shepherd the members there even though public evangelism as such remained impossible.

Florence's spirits rose with the prospect of living in the mission house in Istanbul, high up on a cliff overlooking the Bosporous on one side and the Golden Horn on the other—that spit of land where the sultans had kept their harems. From the house, one could look right out over the turrets and domes of the church of Hagia Sophia. Beautiful Istanbul—home of emperors and princes. It still trailed remnants of past glories.

The Osters' predecessors in Istanbul had been the Klinger family, now transferred to Jerusalem. Delays over visas and waiting for the birth of the Klingers' first baby, however, gave time for the two couples to get well acquainted.

At the Klingers' farewell party Florence had her first introduction to real Turkish gentility. According to custom, each guest in a home must be given a teaspoonful of preserves, jam, or fudge. It is conveyed on a long-handled spoon suspended over a glass of water to catch the drops. Each guest licks the spoon clean, and then drinks the water. Florence felt squeamish about the sanitary aspects of the gesture and at the prospect of having to swallow that much sugar in one gulp. Nonetheless, the fifty church members who attended the party presented the Klingers with a set of these graceful, long-handled spoons. Their memories of those many years of service obviously were sweet ones, and Florence felt warm and at home among these people—their new congregation.

The Osters found that *"Turkish* Turkish" was quite different from the Turkish dialect they had learned in Persia. Assuming too much of her Azerbaijani Turkish, Florence made more than one error. The young people in the Istanbul church immediately wanted to learn English, and they quickly coaxed Florence into teaching them. They would come to her home, but on which day? *"Doshamba galma chunke mashgul am, Seshamba bekar am,"* she told them. They convulsed in laughter. "What did I say," she asked.

"You said," they chortled, " 'On Monday I am busy and on Tuesday I am unmarried.' "

Florence joined in the fun. "I was wrong. I'm always married—even on Tuesdays."

Frank and Florence had no more than settled into their top-floor, grand-view apartment, however, than alarming news came from Kenneth. In a routine health check during his freshman year at college, he had been diagnosed as having tuberculosis. He had already gone down to Indiana to stay with his uncle and aunt and take the full rest treatment—the only known cure for the disease at that time. "But don't worry," he wrote to his parents. "Instead, do this: Pray and trust God . . . who will do all things right."

Black fear groped its way into Florence's heart. A third child? And neither she nor Frank could be with him. The next news, however, sounded much better. The specialists in Indianapolis had decreed that he had done so well that he would need to stay in bed only three months. At the end of that time, the best news of all came. Since he had already missed out on the rest of the current school year, the General Conference planned to send him home to Istanbul for vacation.

Florence felt jubilant over this generous offer. Nothing she had ever received in all their six years in Turkey meant more to her than Kenneth's homecoming.

But even in the midst of their supreme moment of rejoicing, with Frank, Florence, and most of the Istanbul church members down on the docks to wave Kenneth into the pier—it happened. Just as the gangplank came down, newsboys rushed down to the ship waving their headliners and shouting, *"Nihayet harb bashladi* [Finally war has come]."

Over the next few days, in between war-news bulletins, Kenneth inserted happier accounts of how Uncle Omer had taken him to New York, how they had attended the World's Fair just before he got on the Beirut-bound boat, and how great the new radio was that he had brought with him. The radio was the first the Osters had ever owned, and the possibility of hearing instantly what was going on around the world enthralled them.

Huddling over the radio listening to the news became a family routine. The names of Neville Chamberlain and Adolph Hitler and all the rest crackled in over the air waves and became household words.

Into the Storm

What would come to be labeled World War II unleashed its fury on the world. For some who had spent the intervening years in hard places, it seemed merely to be a continuation of World War I. In any case, for Frank and Florence their lot had improved—they were much less isolated than they had been twenty-five years earlier. The wonderful radio not only kept them up-to-the-last-minute on the war developments, but also tempered that news with beautiful classical music from Rome and other cultural centers. News from the family front, on the other hand, came irregularly, the miles being hopelessly disrupted again.

Frank and Florence had been grandparents for some months already before a letter came from Winton and Dorothy confirming the arrival of Linda Lou, the first grandchild. Things like that frustrated Florence, for she longed to share these personal family moments at firsthand. And once in a while the gnawing question recurred: "Really, what are we accomplishing here in Turkey at this time?"

In 1940 ominous news on the home front vied with the war and even the grandchild for attention. A colossal earthquake devastated northeast Turkey, sending 40,000 people into eternity. The floods that poured in immediately afterward killed another 1200. Relief work again! The church members in Istanbul did what they could—food baskets went to several homes. The peas, beans, lentils, rice, raisins, nuts, potatoes, onions, and olive oil—every item represented a sacrifice on one side, and a bulwark against starvation on the other. Even a few oranges got through as a very special treat.

As the months went by, life resolved itself into a triangle: the war, Frank's low-key efforts at evangelism, and Kenneth's impatience to get back to school. In February, eleven months after Ken had dropped out of college, the General Conference studied his latest chest X-rays and approved his return to Emmanuel Missionary College. Travel across the Mediterranean was uncertain in every way. A devastating winter storm laid him up in Malta for two weeks and gave him cause to recall the Apostle Paul who had wintered there for a like reason 1800 years before. A New York-bound ship finally made it into the Atlantic and on to the United States. Kenneth picked up where he had left off at school; and Frank and Florence settled into the uncertain routine of living on the perimeters of the uproar among their warring neighbors.

The pendulum swung between the spiritual highs of mission service and the terrifying lows of war. First came to case of Erica Cholak and her husband, Hemdy Bey. The beautiful Erica had a colorful, international past. Polish by birth, and German by reason of her career as an actress, she'd married a Turk. As for religion, she had been a Seventh-day Adventist for some years in Switzerland. When her husband's business failed, and he returned with their little daughter to live at home in Istanbul, she signed a film-making contract in Berlin. Once again in Switzerland, however, she watched those whom she knew must be Sabbath keepers on their way to church in Lausanne. On a compulsion she followed them, and almost within the hour she rejected her former life, canceled all engagements, and was rebaptized. Her return to her husband and daughter in Istanbul dramatically renewed her home and marriage. It took until three a.m. the first night for her to explain it all to her Moslem husband. Highly pleased with the changes he saw in her, Hemdy began to reorder his own life to match. As for the church, the little Istanbul company welcomed Erica's bright, warm presence into their midst.

Meanwhile, news flashes about the "Big Bully" (Adolph Hitler) became daily fare. After a brave defiance that won world admiration, little Finland went down in proud surrender. Foreign embassies urged their citizens to evacuate, and the Turks read great black headlines warning them to prepare for the worst. Should war come to Turkey, girls of fifteen and grandmothers of sixty-five, and all the women in between, would be drafted into military service.

Frank's modest little Sunday night meetings continued. Very few people came—about four or five, to be exact. And yet the night that young Simon Fasulacian decided to be baptized it was a reward of the kind that made the effort, the frustration, and the loneliness bearable.

Next, Denmark fell to the victorious forces of the Third Reich. Frank and Florence hung over the radio nightly and followed Hitler's triumphal entry into Norway. "Do you think, Frank," Florence ventured one night, "that we should think of evacuating? The news all this week has been uniformly bad."

Frank looked up, almost surprised. "Why Floss— God will show us what to do when that time comes. You know that."

Florence felt the familiar surge of hopelessness and discouragement swelling up over her horizons again. "How will we . . . ?"

"Courage, my dear," Frank smiled, recognizing her very real fears. "It's quite possible that some very particular work remains for us to do here. And we wouldn't want to leave that undone, would we?"

"No, of course, not." Florence felt a familiar tightness in her throat. But with Frank beside her, she would keep faith. When the time came they would know what to do.

The next Sabbath she saw Edward and his widowed mother arrive at church, along with a couple of his former school friends. After his baptism the previous summer, he had become strangely and violently ill. After forty days in the hospital, he came out and began selling books and tracts. He had done remarkably well, and for young people like that who still needed counsel and leadership, Florence knew in her inmost soul that they still had a work to do.

One morning three days later, Florence heard a frantic pounding on the door of the mission house. She found Edward, broken and in tears, terrified of something unseen and unknown. "Edward!" She pulled him through the doorway. His legs almost gave way under him, and Frank had to help him upstairs.

"Tell us, Edward! Whatever happened?" When the boy could control his voice, he explained. "I was selling books down at the bridge, and—and the police—they took me."

"But why?" Florence's ire arose. She knew he had permission to sell those certain little books and tracts in the city.

"Yes, but I wasn't supposed to be in *that* place. And they—Oh, they beat me. So many stripes—for a long time. My back—"

"Why, you poor child!" Florence jumped up. "Look at his back, Frank, and I'll prepare the bath." The faint, broken young man aroused Florence's sympathetic impulses immediately and completely.

After a bath, rest, and a good hot dinner, Edward was ready to go again. "Thank you. Oh, thank you, *Atam va Anam* [my father and mother]. Now I have strength again."

The Osters watched Edward with his little bag of tracts, heading off down the street again, back to colporteuring. "Edward is real 'quality.'" Florence looked after the retreating figure of her Turkish "son."

"Yes, Floss. For those like him we must stay as long as we can."

A few weeks later Frank had to go to court himself. Unlike Edward, he paid in cash instead of pain. The controversy centered on their precious radio. When Ken had brought it in and paid customs taxes on it, they had naturally assumed that by doing so they had permission enough for using it. But not so. Radios could not be operated in Turkey without a license. Their ignorance of this law made no difference. And to add to the enormity of the misdemeanor, the registration of the radio had not been transferred from Kenneth's name to theirs.

Finally, Frank paid the fine, worked through the red tape, accumulated all the necessary documents, and came home triumphant. "Well, Floss," he announced as he set his briefcase down and loosened his tie. "Almost time for the news again. And tonight we can hear it *legally!*"

"Good." Florence sat down in her favorite rocking chair while Frank tuned in the radio. "But, I fear, legality isn't going to improve the quality of what we have to hear."

And it didn't. Hilter's blitzkrieg swept across Europe, gaining victory after victory. Now Belgium had surrendered. Who could tell where the Axis powers would strike next?

Letters from home that made the Atlantic crossing safely and also survived the mutilation of the censors, voiced one anxious question: "Aren't you planning to come home?"

Alone with herself and God, Florence struggled with that question and those letters. Clearly Frank had no notion of going home.

She had spoken to him so often about being out in the field so long, away from the children and family. The dangers of war were, of course, self-evident and needed no commentary on her part. But he always objected. "Really, he's so well and strong and so full of courage; one can't blame him," she wrote to Vandella. And yet, he was almost sixty years old. Surely the idea of going home *could* be a legitimate thought by now.

And what of her own courage? Well, that had become the daily battle she had to fight. By and large, her faith lifted her up and carried her over the vast chasms of despair. So in the next line she wrote: "In a couple of weeks we're going to have a baptism for three young women, and maybe some others. Several are studying but are not quite ready." Even in the darkest hours she managed to keep in perspective the great mission to which she had given her life. She stayed by her task even when her very soul cried out for the fellowship of home and children.

Now Rumania had fallen into German hands. In other words, the enemy now stood right on Turkey's northern border. Tension, suspicion, restrictions, privation—Turkey's taut nerves tightened up still more.

But the baptism for the four young people shone like a flame in the dark tunnel for Frank and Florence. The Protestant church where they rented a side room would not permit a baptistery. Florence's creativity carried off the day, all the same. Frank had a very large tub made and placed in the church, and she decorated it with green vines and white flowers. The beauty of the service and the singing of the young people impressed many observers who, in turn, expressed a desire to participate as soon as possible. And so, by one's, two's, and four's the little Istanbul church grew, in quality steadily making up for what it lacked in numbers.

On October 28, 1940, Italy declared war on Greece. Now the conflict had truly reached Turkey's doorstep. Because of the treaties she had with her neighbors, it seemed only a matter of time before the storm sucked her in too.

"If war hits Istanbul, Frank, just about the whole city will go up in flames," Florence said as they switched off the radio to brood over the latest news.

"Yes, the wooden frame buildings still fill whole districts, even though further construction has been forbidden. Istanbul has such a long, hot history of devastating fires. It'll be bad, if it comes."

Florence got up to make the rounds and adjust the blackout curtains Frank had recently devised. If one ray of light strayed out on the street, it could bring the police and severe punishment to their door instantly. Frank's curtain invention, like everything he undertook, was near-perfect in precision and efficiency; so their privacy and that of the mission remained unviolated.

Still, Turkey seemed to be roller-coasting into war. Many of the city schools moved to country locations, and free railroad tickets were provided for city dwellers who wanted to evacuate into the interior. They could take with them whatever would fit within the fifty-kilo luggage allowance, and no more.

The Osters pondered just what they should do. In early January, 1941, they received thirty-five pieces of mail. Florence reveled in these mail floods, as she had many years before in Persia. This time, however, one ordinary-appearing letter from the General Conference held a real surprise. It called them to move to Basra, southern Iraq. By the end of the month another letter arrived to confirm the appointment.

No, it wasn't to go home, but it did promise rescue out of the hot spot. For the time being, it seemed, the decision had been made for them. Florence wished it could have been home, but she took up the challenge with courage. Maybe Frank had been right after all. Something must still remain to be done, *now,* out in this tumultuous part of the world. While they waited for the Syrian visa to come through, Florence mentally packed, sorted, and sold the household goods in anticipation of the reality which she supposed would come. Erica Cholak wanted to buy everything they had to sell, so that part could be quite simple.

Meanwhile, inundated by the grief of war, Greece had been catapulted into a terrible nation-wide famine. Another letter came from the General Conference. It asked Frank to secure permission to go into Greece to bring relief and money to the stricken workers and church members. Frank immediately opened negotiations with the German consul in Istanbul, and Florence shelved plans for moving. Her role in the next act of the drama would clearly be that of "holding the fort." Because of his Swiss citizenship it was at least theoretically possible for Frank to get into Greece. He studied his Swiss passport with satisfaction. "How fortunate that I never gave this up."

"And how fortunate too," Florence added, "that snug little Switzerland has managed to keep out of this whole mess—both times!"

Negotiations stretched out through days, into weeks, and then months. The Osters prayed daily for the plight of the church in Greece, for whom every day of delay must mean suffering and perhaps even death. Finally, at the end of six months, Frank had it all together. The transit visa for Bulgaria (a nation which had been acting hostile of late), and an entry visa for Greece. Then he had a whole fistful of other permits and papers for the journey. Also, the money had arrived safely from America—all $2000 of it.

The long, intervening weeks gave the Armenian Greek church members—and others—in Istanbul time to learn that Frank would go to Greece. They came to him in droves. The list of names and addresses, the quantities of money, the packages of food, and the weight of love and concern grew into a mountain of responsibility. Frank coped with it in his characteristic way. He made a little columnized notebook in which he recorded all these vital statistics.

Florence spent hours working on the little book that would be the bridge between concerned senders and needy receivers. Frank converted all the money into U. S. greenbacks—presumably the most negotiable currency. Florence spent most of the night before his departure copying every serial number on the bills into his little notebook.

"I'm going to have to keep my own needs very modest," he said, as he surveyed the quantities of flour, powdered milk, dried fish, and other edibles that made up almost the whole of his baggage. "But for me it's only a matter of days—for them it's been months."

For the past five weeks Frank had almost daily expected to be able to leave. Florence had even made a lunch for him several times, all in vain. But now she watched the train pull out of the Istanbul station with her Frank aboard—and she knew he was really gone. This time she felt a greater emptiness than she had ever known on any of his previous missions. He expected to be back in about a week, but he said, "Don't start worrying about me for at least a month. Who can tell?"

The first part of the journey promised to be relatively

predictable—in Sophia, Bulgaria, he would leave the train and transfer to a German plane, which would fly him into Athens. Florence considered, parenthetically, how Frank's plane flight would mark a new phase in the progress of missions and in the arrangement of their personal affairs, as well. The beginning of a new kind of life, no doubt.

Very tired from the stress of the past twenty-four hours, Florence decided to treat herself to the luxury of an afternoon nap when she got back to the apartment. She had just taken off her hat when she saw it, lying in plain view on Frank's desk. His little notebook! She had forgotten to return it to him after she had entered the last address! How could she have been so careless! All introspective thoughts of rest fled as a charge of shock and anxiety shot through her. Whatever could Frank do without the book? How on earth could she ever send it to him? Both questions seemed to have no answer. Neither she nor Frank *did* things like this. And now—"

Calling a car, she hurried down to the German consul. Frank had practically lived there over the past six months, but she arrived a stranger. The explaining took much time. "He *must* have this notebook," she concluded. "Without it he can do nothing when he gets to Greece."

The consul took the precious little notebook and studied it with care. "What is the meaning of all these names?"

"Those are the people to whom he is to give the money and food," Florence answered, certain that she had already said that at least four times—but the consul had plenty of time.

"Ah, so! And why all the numbers?" He had reached the money pages now.

Florence reviewed her case again. "They are the serial numbers for the money he's carrying."

The consul retired into a back office with unknown and unseen dignitaries, who no doubt could have much influence on the course of events. Florence looked out the window, paced the floor, and prayed. Somehow God would have to get Frank and his notebook together.

When he finally returned to give the verdict, the consul was smiling; and Florence took heart. In fact, he appeared now to be a very nice man indeed. "Yes, Frau Oster, I think we can get this book to Herr Oster."

Shortly he introduced Florence to a German *fräulein* scheduled to leave that evening for Berlin. Handing the notebook to the woman, the consul said, "Take this with you and deliver it to Herr Oster, this lady's husband, when you arrive in Sophia."

"And how shall I know him?" A logical question!

The consul thought a moment. "Oh, just wave the book, and he'll recognize it and ask for it."

"But, Herr Consul," she countered, "the guards at the station would suspect something. They would arrest me for collaborating with the enemy."

"True! Then how—?" The consul seemed to have exhausted his supply of ideas.

Florence listened to the trend of the conversation with growing anxiety. Surely, it wouldn't fail now! Then a wholly unpremeditated idea sprang into her mind, as if by external implant. "I have an idea! Let her keep the notebook hidden in her purse. I'll go home and get a copy of our church paper, the *Review and Herald*. My husband will recognize the paper immediately."

The consul looked at her with approval—no, even admiration perhaps. "Excellent," he said. "I'll send instructions to Herr Oster now to meet this lady at the Sophia train station."

So the jigsaw puzzle was pieced together, at least from Florence's end of it.

For Frank, more obstacles barred the way. Still, before the next testing time came, he had the sensational experience of standing in the bustling Sophia station and seeing a Nazi girl flaunting a copy of the dear old familiar *Review* over the heads of the crowd. In moments he had the notebook in his hands again. *"Danke! Vielen, vielen Dank, Fräulein* [Many thanks, lady!"] He looked up into the smoky girders of the station. "And thank you *too,* Lord!" He knew God stood in constant attendance upon his project of relief and rescue.

All the same, the flight to Athens could be no simple, walk-on affair. Not with the vast amount of luggage he had. A visa in hand still didn't insure his getting aboard a plane to Greece, with that handicap. Then he remembered a Roman Catholic priest he had met years before in Germany, and he decided to seek his advice. The priest listened to his description of his situation and concluded that the endeavor should be worth his interest. "I do have some influence here," he said. "Come with me."

They went out to the airport. Frank couldn't determine the exact nature of the priest's "influence," but whatever it was, it worked. In no time, he had a seat for Frank on a direct flight to Athens, and his baggage was checked through.

"Thank you!" Frank now had to go into the immigration office for the examination of his passport. "You have helped me very much. Many starving people will benefit from your kindness."

The passport examination proved to be irritatingly long and deliberate. While he waited, Frank heard a plane land, and then a while later, take off again. Only a little time remained before his scheduled departure hour, and Frank grew restless. "I've been waiting a very long time for my passport," he told the officers. "My plane is going to leave very soon."

The men regarded him with mild interest. "Where are you going?"

"To Athens."

"Athens! Hah! That plane arrived ahead of time and has just left. Look!" They pointed out the window to the south. "There it goes over the top of the mountain now."

"Oh, no! No!" Usually organized and in control, Frank felt surprise and shock bordering on hysteria. "I have lots of goods on that plane! Much of it is perishable. I *must* go!"

It was a valiant gesture, but the plane had just about disappeared over the ragged skyline by now. He still stood helplessly on the ground. Suddenly, he sensed someone just behind him. The priest! "I wanted to see you safely off, so I waited," he said. "I see it was to a purpose."

A hasty exchange between the priest and the officers transpired—force on the side of the priest and submission of the side of the men. Frank stared dumfounded as the chief picked up the telephone and ordered the plane back to the airport. The priest's intervention—it worked again. He had asked for a miracle, and now he saw it happen. The aircraft circled and returned to land in Sophia again. Escorted to the plane like a VIP, he joined his precious cargo aboard.

The flight to Greece gave Frank time to review with God again the potential difficulties of entering the country with so much merchandise and money. He knew that prolonged questioning would be a regular part of the entry process, all in the name of security. He well knew that some questions, if answered directly, would jeopardize his success. He determined not to compromise his honesty, no matter what.

Last to board in Sophia, and now the last to disembark in Athens, Frank approached the checkpoint turnstile. Just at the moment a scuffle erupted at the far end of the customs building—a fight between Greek and German officials. Everyone in the building seemed to have a vested interest in either one side or the other; so the whole crowd converged on that end of the room to watch the outcome of the mini-war. Frank found himself entirely alone at the empty window. So he simply walked across the barrier zone and arrived safely in Greece, no questions asked.

His unrestricted visa permitted him to exchange his money at 300 drachmas to the dollar instead of the current local rate of only 3 lira to the dollar. The money ballooned into an enormous sum. Although the visas had been late in coming, they had in fact come through just at the crucial time when Frank could bring the greatest possible blessing to the Greek church. Obviously, God's time clock had been set for just this sequence of events. "And, Pastor Oster," Elder Christoforides, the mission director said, "do you know that we didn't have *any* money left to pay our workers' wages this coming week!"

The famine conditions appalled Frank—and he was no novice in such things. Estimates showed that about 1000 people starved to death daily in the city. "Moreover," the pastor said, "when babies and children die, they aren't buried properly. Often they're thrown into garbage cans so that the death is unreported and the family can still collect their food coupons."

Frank spent all day Friday with the pastor and other workers preparing sacks of rice, flour, and other food. The church floor was covered wall-to-wall with food bags, each identified according to the size of the family.

He would never forget the next day when everyone came to church and all were invited into the anteroom to claim their packages. Later, when he got home, he described in detail to Florence how the people wept and prayed and said, "Manna from heaven, truly!" Then they all went back into the church, the treasures cradled in their arms, and thanked God for His wonderful provision for them. The rest of the time passed in sharing their experiences of hardship, trials of faith, and providential deliverances. Frank thought the recital of the marvels of divine love would never end.

One lady dentist described graphically how the Germans had requisitioned huge quantities of flour, so that very little remained for the people. Still, from her own three-fourth-empty flour bin she began to share what she had with two or three families every day. "And do you know," she declared with tears standing in her eyes, "that every time I go back to my flour barrel it's *full?*"

"Amen! Praise God!" The fervent chorus went up from the congregation.

"Dear sister, you are of course, a modern widow of Zarepath, aren't you?" Frank said.

"Yes, pastor, I am. And to think that God chose *me!*"

But the joy went far beyond the food. Frank became a one-man communication center, a crossroads of information between the friends in Istanbul and the beleaguered Greeks and Armenians in Athens. By constant reference to his notebook, he managed to keep all the messages straight, and with the help of the local pastor he located every name on his long, long list.

Because of his providential and highly unusual entry into the country, Frank was able to stay three full weeks instead of the 8 days prescribed by his visa. Then, loaded with messages-in-return, love and greetings—but no food—Frank returned to Istanbul.

Tired and drawn and twelve pounds leaner than when he left, he arrived home. Florence wept with sheer relief. "But Floss!" Frank soothed. "I told you not to start to worry about me until one month!"

"I know, but I couldn't help it." Florence looked up at her husband. It took almost all of the first night for Florence to hear of Frank's marvelous and obviously divinely directed adventures. And at breakfast the next morning Frank looked even more worn than he had the night before.

"Frank, you look so utterly exhausted." His haggard gauntness frightened Florence more than she would admit. "Couldn't we possibly take a little vacation somewhere, just for a few days?"

Frank sighed. "Yes, Floss, that's exactly what I'd like to do. In fact, we ought to do it. But not yet. I have to go through my whole trip in reverse. So many people want to know about their families in Greece."

"You're right, of course," Florence replied. "How can you blame all these people—all these war-divided families. They've not had—and may not have again—any chance to get messages through. Who knows when it will change?"

"Even the Swiss consul here in Istanbul has been unable to get news of the more than sixty Swiss families living in Greece, so I will spend a good deal of time with him too."

"Isn't it amazing," Florence said, "how you've crossed all these political borders and war zones and never once been intercepted or questioned?"

"Of course," Frank replied, "my mission was, as it always has been, a special one. As a pastor, and with God's guidance and protection, I could do what perhaps no other person in Turkey could have done."

On an afternoon in October, they stood on the balcony of their apartment overlooking the harbor. Florence remarked, "We've heard nothing more about the call to Iraq."

"No, we haven't. That, Floss, might well be a plan that's run aground for us permanently."

Florence looked at Frank sharply. How she would like to have read his inmost thoughts at that point! She wondered how he would consider an order to evacuate if it came now. But instead she watched the evening fishing boats put out to sea. "Anyway, Frank, I think we both know why we had a delay. We've identified that special work that only you could have done." She had to admit now that God had had a hand in it all.

Frank drew her close. "Yes, Floss. It's a wonderful, dove-tailed pattern to look back upon now. And as for the future—it'll be all right too."

"Of course. And about the future—the immediate future," Florence chimed in. "Remember that vacation? Why couldn't we take it now?"

Frank's unusually prompt response startled her. "Yes, Floss. Why not?"

A Destiny Fulfilled

The two-week vacation cruise on the Black Sea which Frank arranged lived up to the best in recreational ideals. The possibility of doing such a thing, in itself seemed a miracle to Florence. Leisure at such a time? They got round-trip tickets that took them all the way to the eastern end of Turkey, to within eighteen miles of Batumi. The war seemed to be a conflict on some other planet—something they acknowledged intellectually, but which for the moment at least, had nothing to do with them. Good food, beautiful golden days, plenty of rest—the healing process worked in body, mind, and spirit.

Frank gained back two of the pounds he had lost, but Florence did better. "Frank!" she exclaimed one morning, as she fastened her belt into its last hole. "I'm getting fat!"

Frank laughed. "No harm, sweetheart. You can use it!"

"Well, so could you. Why can't we divide it up more evenly."

"I couldn't answer that one," Frank admitted. "I guess that's your problem."

The trip produced but one flutter of excitement to remind everyone that the fallout of war still oppressed even under the sunny skies over the Black Sea. Two small boats appeared on the starboard side of their ship. After the captain signaled and received no reply, he ordered some of his crew to board them and investigate. Their findings only deepened the mystery. The boats were heavily equipped: plenty of gasoline, first-aid supplies, field glasses, and clothing. The more sinister cargo consisted of many rounds of ammunition and a bomb. Not a soul was aboard. Under the curious gaze of the passengers, the ship's big winches hoisted the pair of Russian boats onto the deck. The mystery of the deserted boats remained unsolved—one more dark secret of war intrigue.

When Frank and Florence got back to Istanbul, they needed all the courage and resources they had laid up in store during their holidays. It took but one session of the evening radio newscast to realize that things were *not* good. Bulgaria had been invaded, and German troops now approached Turkish borders. Rumors of the German invasion filled the city—and Turkey would have welcomed the Axis powers gladly. Hallmarks of war appeared everywhere, and food supplies had declined measurably. Cheerful news certainly was in short supply. The word that Winton had passed his National Board examinations and had now become a "real doctor" was one of the few things they had to rejoice over.

A cable arrived from the General Conference. It read: "Advise evacuation to United States." Florence looked at the paper. Here it was—the message that she had expected, pondered over, yes, even courted for months. It meant going home.

Now, however, instead of feeling exuberant, she scarcely knew what she felt. Frank's reaction would be predictable. Duty and service would still dominate his mind, regardless of where the orders came from.

"But, Floss," he argued. "We stayed in Persia all through World War I. We never thought of evacuation."

"True, but maybe this war isn't just like every other war," Florence suggested.

"But famine and all the other distress—" Frank went on. "We've survived that and been able to relieve thousands of helpless people too at those times."

The Osters kept their regular date with the evening news and discussed evacuation day after day, from all angles. But they held back on actual preparations to leave. Neither of them had reached the point of admitting that their long years of mission service would end in unceremonious flight. "Somehow it just doesn't seem that it can be *right,*" Frank said, as he worried the subject around again for the hundredth time. To give in and leave? The very thought went against every fiber in his system. A second cable came from the General Conference, repeating the instructions of the first.

By the time the third cable arrived, ordering immediate evacuation, Frank and Florence had won one of the hardest battles of their lives. "We can't ignore it any longer, Floss. We must go." Frank spoke with calmness and control.

"*Inshallah,*" Florence whispered. "It must be time."

"Yes, Floss, it *must* be God's will," Frank mused. "We have evidence on every side. It would be wrong to resist." The decision to leave was infinitely more difficult than the decision to come.

After preliminary investigation Frank came home to announce that they would likely have to leave Istanbul by air. "We'll have to get rid of everything."

"The lighter we travel, the easier the journey," Florence agreed. A fleeting recollection of "Egypt to Canaan" crossed her mind as she tried to decide what should go into their four suitcases.

As for giving up all her possessions, she could accept that part of the venture calmly. Anyone who had torn up their home as many times as she had; and who had sold out, replaced, and given away everything as often as she had done, would not be unduly disturbed by one more move. But this would be the cleanest break of all—emotionally as well as materially.

They shipped their entire library to Middle East College in Beirut, Lebanon, and then put what they could up for sale. Whatever remained had to be given away. After the stripping down was complete and the heartbreaking farewells had been made, Frank discovered that air evacuation was no longer possible. A train through Syria and Palestine and down to Egypt would now be the only escape. "Well," Florence sighed. "Perhaps we could have kept a *few* things after all!" But what was done was done, and possessions were a small matter at this point anyway.

In the manner of all those who must flee from war zones, Frank and Florence arrived days later in Cairo, tired and with nothing more than what they carried in their hands. Worse than that, the emotional upheaval of loss and separation and the frustration of a task unfinished left them with a gnawing emptiness which not even the prospect of home and family could fully allay. The quietness, hospitality and relative security of the Heliopolis home of their hosts, the E. L. Bransons, soothed and warmed.

"I think I've found something for you," Elder Branson announced after several days of investigation. "A small liberty boat will join a convoy in the Suez and sail for New York in three or four weeks. I believe we're going to get you a place on it."

The Osters thanked Elder Branson, but Florence felt almost too weary to register any feeling. All had to rest in hands stronger than hers. After a few days they felt equal to some sightseeing. Even though the war raged above and around and now all through the desert, the memorials of ancient Egypt stood unaffected and oblivious. Hatshepsut's temples at Karnak, the millennia-old tombs of kings and queens, the predictable cycles of the great Nile River, the priceless funeral treasures and their mummified owners—all spoke of a long-gone, static society impervious to change and the terrors of a mere few rounds of bullets. Somehow this sightseeing helped get things back into perspective.

Also supporting this refreshingly different view of life were the pleasant Sabbaths when the nature of work in the Egypt Mission could be most fully appreciated. Early in the morning fifteen or twenty Adventist American soldiers would converge on the Branson home. Some walked from encampments just outside the city, others found rides, and still others came in by plane. Breakfast for the whole crowd preceded going to church in Heliopolis.

Then Mrs. Branson engineered marvelous vegetarian dinners. Afterward everyone sat around and shared experiences. Not one person present lacked "experiences"—most of them of a very inspiring sort. Back to the church for young people's meeting, and then home to Bransons for supper and sundown worship. Homecooked meals and Christian fellowship gave the whole day its momentum. Florence decided she had never had before, and perhaps would never have again, Sabbath just like this. The friendship and fun made the soldiers reluctant to leave. After sundown, they started off to their barracks, but now they seemed to have lead in their boots.

Finally the day came when the Osters joined the convoy—a dull gray company of thirty-one camouflaged ships. Extravagant precautions had to be taken for safety reasons. Before sailing, the passengers had to learn by heart all of the ship's signals. Their life jackets had to be constantly within arm's reach, and they wore whistles pinned to their clothes, to make their own signals if they went overboard. The passenger vessels wore low skirts of netting to catch underwater missiles, while from the top mast of each one sailed a large balloon designed to deter low-flying aircraft.

Although the balloons had been a hopeful idea, a bad storm the second day at sea tore away all but two of them. Worse still, the Osters' ship lost its rudder and had to drop back from the main group until repairs could be made. Florence looked at the convoy ahead, zig-zagging across the mine-infested Mediterranean, and felt very much like the lost sheep, far out of the fold. What a relief when their straggling ship could rejoin the group, ringed around again with the escorting warships.

All the way to Gibraltar the convoy hugged the north coast of Africa. Often the long whistle blew to warn of imminent air attack. Passengers and crew alike had to pull on their life jackets and scuttle up to the lifeboat stations, almost all in one movement. The days followed one another in active, exciting succession. "On alert" became a round-the-clock situation and left little time for leisure living. Out beyond Gibraltar the convoy split, some ships sailing north to Liverpool and London, but the main body moving on across the Atlantic.

The long anxious days, though filled with activity, also prompted long, long thoughts—thoughts which stretched backward, forward, and upward. The makeup of the convoy itself challenged the imagination. Frank and Florence often discussed the motley, oddly assorted collection of ocean-going vessels—liberty boats, merchant marines, destroyers, freighters, in all sizes and shapes. Each contained its own community of passengers and crew, strangers who had been thrown together under most threatening circumstances. Amid all the great diversity, however, the common danger demanded close unity, discipline, and complete harmony of action. As all shared the fear and the terror, so all hoped and waited—and many prayed—for the common goal of home and safety.

"It's a parable of the kingdom, Floss," Frank concluded.

A brand new insight flooded through Florence. "And Frank, do you know," she said, "the average speed of the whole convoy can be no faster than the top speed of the slowest ship!"

"Of course, Floss," Frank dropped the life jacket he carried over his arm and pulled Florence close. "In heaven's homecoming we must all arrive together."

Florence mulled over the parable further. It was not just of the kingdom but of their own lifework too. They had given thirty-five years of their lives to the pioneering of the most ancient lands in the world. There had been high points and many low ones too. And in retrospect it seemed that much time and energy had been given for pitifully small results. Small, if one were to consider just the numbers. And yet, surely, in God's great time clock there would be a way and a time—somehow, somewhere—for the very slowest ship to come into port.

Finally the Statue of Liberty loomed up, a silhouette in the morning fog, and two more missionaries knew that they had reached home. Florence studied Frank as he hunched over the railing, studying the great gray shapes which were New York City. "We've done our best, Floss. All the years. I'm satisfied now, for we gave all we had."

Dear Frank! How hard it was to let go. "Of course, you did. And now the rest of the work must lie with others."

As if crossing the bridge in one stride, Frank straightened up. "We have only to thank God for safety and for the blessing of a new task to take up here at home." He smiled now. "We've arrived."

Florence watched the foam-flecked waves eddy back into the ship's wake. "Inshallah," she said. "By God's direction, we've done it."

The words pronounced a benediction upon their lifetime of overseas service.

Epilogue

For the Osters the break between their overseas years and the work that followed in the homeland brought the same radical changes which every long-time missionary must undergo. The greater his commitment, the larger his adjustments. The many pleasant features of the homecoming offset much of the trauma of transition.

Frank transplanted his organizational and witnessing energies to Indiana, where he pastored four churches and three companies in the Logansport area for the four years remaining before retirement. And now Florence could at last satisfy her craving to partake in all the family "rites of passage." When Ken married Dorothy Nelson in Takoma Park, Maryland, in 1945, the groom's parents were there along with everyone else. Dorothy's father, Dr. Andrew Nelson, performed the ceremony. And as the daughter of pioneer missionaries to the Orient, she considered going back to Persia with Kenneth the most natural thing in the world to do. In carrying on the work that Frank and Florence began, Ken and Dorothy have gone on to achieve their own foreign-mission service record of more than thirty years in the Middle East. Ken has used his lifetime acquaintance with the local languages and culture to cultivate new approaches to the Moslem world. Winton, by this time had established his medical practice in San Diego.

The full, busy years passed, but never so busy that Frank and Florence lost their connection with the people and the concerns of the land to which they had given their youth, their health, and the best years of their lives. In 1950 they retired to live near Winton in San Diego, California.

Between 1960 and 1964 Florence had to go through the valley of the shadow three times. Frank fell prey to a lingering, painful illness, and Florence passed through that ultimate sorrow—the kind of loss which can be known only by a woman who has loved, supported, and stood by her husband in lonely times and places when he had no one else but his God and her. After Frank died in November, 1960, Florence spent the following year in Beirut, Lebanon, with Ken and Dorothy. Living again among the people and places she had loved, helped her heart to heal.

Her sister Vandella died in Ventura Estates, California. She was the one whose loving interest and newsy letters had sustained Florence through so many dark hours over the years. Then Winton went to Switzerland, that unforgettable country to which both family roots and teenage memories had always tied him. He wanted to visit Frutigen, the alpine town where his father had been born. On the way, however, he died in a mountain-climbing accident, and Florence mourned again the loss of her eldest. He was on the way, she feels, to fulfilling his dream of working as a doctor in Persia, an ambition which had never left him.

Today you could find Florence in a senior citizens' home in Loma Linda, California; while her one remaining son, Ken, and his wife live in Shiraz, south Iran. In the city which lies within the ancient neighborhood of the summer palace of Cyrus the Great, they work—the only Seventh-day Adventist missionaries within 350 miles. They pioneer again, and the "family pattern" recurs.

As for Florence, the years have dimmed her eyes now, but not her clear insight into the things of the spirit. The fragility of her ninety-one years and the uncertainty of the beat of her tired heart belie the stoutness of her faith and the keenness of her mind. In her warm, outgoing personality and lively enthusiasm, it's not at all hard to see again that girl who gave her life to God and Persia more than seventy years ago.

Alone now with her memories, she might well dwell on her losses, and they have been many. Instead, however, she claims anew that promise of Isaiah 43:5.

"Fear not: for I am with thee: I will bring thy seed from the east, and gather thee from the west; I will say to the north, Give up; and to the south, Keep not back: bring my sons from far, and my daughters from the ends of the earth."

She thinks of the four graves at the "ends of the earth"—little Winona in the east, Iran; Francis in the west, Michigan; Winton in the north, Switzerland; and Frank in the south, San Diego. But she has no fear, for the God whom she has served so long will redeem His promise and restore her family in His good time. Furthermore, she has a multitude of other sons and daughters scattered around the world. Except for the loving care of *Khanoom* and *Agha* Oster they might never have understood the meaning of the Christian life.

Has the burden been too great? Was the price of it all too high? Could Florence have given her life and talents to some better cause? *No,* she will tell you—a thousand times, *no!* Living in total commitment to God's will for all of these years, she has seen His guiding hand too many times and has felt His Spirit's soothing comfort too often to wish that anything had been otherwise.

And now, in her late sunset years, she passes her days in that peace and fulfillment which is heaven's gift to all who learn to say, without reservation, *"Inshallah* [If God wills it]."

Dr. Kenneth Oster and his wife, Dorothy, returned to the United States in November of 1979, just prior to the printing of this book.